WARRIOR · 161

TUNNEL RAT IN VIETNAM

GORDON L ROTTMAN

ILLUSTRATED BY BRIAN DELF

Series editor Marcus Cowper

First published in Great Britain in 2012 by Osprey Publishing
Midland House, West Way, Botley, Oxford OX2 0PH, UK
44-02 23rd St, Suite 219, Long Island City, NY 11101, USA
E-mail: info@ospreypublishing.com

OSPREY PUBLISHING IS PART OF THE OSPREY GROUP

A CIP catalog record for this book is available from the British Library

Print ISBN: 978 1 84908 783 4

PDF e-book ISBN: 978 1 84908 784 1

EPUB e-book ISBN: 978 1 78096 042 5

Editorial by Ilios Publishing Ltd, Oxford, UK (www.iliospublishing.com)
Page layout by: Mark Holt
Index by Sandra Shotter
Typeset in Sabon and Myriad Pro
Originated by Blenheim Colour Ltd
Printed in China through Worldprint Ltd

12 13 14 15 16 10 9 8 7 6 5 4 3 2 1

www.ospreypublishing.com

ACKNOWLEDGEMENTS

The author is indebted to Trey Moore of Moore Militaria; David Long of
the Tropic Lightning Museum (25th Infantry Division), Schofield Barracks,
Hawaii; 1st Cavalry Division Museum, Fort Hood, Texas; Frederick Adolphus
of the Fort Polk Museum, Louisiana; and Tom LaeJohn Eli (tunnel rat, 25th
Infantry Division). Special thanks go to Tom Laemlein of Armor Plate Press
for obtaining many of the photographs in this book.

ARTIST'S NOTE

Readers may care to note that the original paintings from which the
colour plates in this book were prepared are available for private sale.
All reproduction copyright whatsoever is retained by the Publishers.
All enquiries should be addressed to:

Brian Delf
7 Burcot Park
Burcot
Abingdon
OX14 3DH
United Kingdom

The Publishers regret that they can enter into no correspondence upon
this matter.

THE WOODLAND TRUST

Osprey Publishing are supporting the Woodland Trust, the UK's leading
woodland conservation charity, by funding the dedication of trees.

MEASUREMENT CONVERSIONS

Imperial measurements are used throughout this book. The following data
will help in converting the imperial measurements to metric.

1 mile = 1.6km
1lb = 0.45kg
1oz = 28g
1 yard = 0.9m
1ft = 0.3m
1in. = 2.54cm/25.4mm
1 gallon = 4.5 liters
1pt = 0.47 liters
1 ton (US) = 0.9 tonnes
1hp = 0.745kW

ABBREVIATIONS

AIT	Advanced Individual Training
ARVN	Army of the Republic of Vietnam (pronounced "Ar-vin")
BCT	Basic Combat Training
C4	a type of plastic explosive
CS	tear gas
MACV	Military Assistance Command, Vietnam (pronounced "Mac-vee")
MOS	Military Occupation Specialty
NCO	non-commissioned officer
NVA	North Vietnamese Army
RVN	Republic of Vietnam (South Vietnam)
VC	Viet Cong

CONTENTS

TUNNEL RAT IN VIETNAM

INTRODUCTION

In 1965, soon after US combat troops had arrived in Vietnam, it was realized that in some areas the Viet Cong (VC) had developed vast tunnel complexes in which to hide from the enemy (see Fortress 48: *Viet Cong & NVA Tunnels/Fortifications of the Vietnam War*, Osprey: Oxford 2006). This was nothing new. It had long been known that such complexes existed, but it was not understood just how extensive they were, their importance to the VC, and how difficult it was to detect and neutralize them.

Most complexes were not nearly as developed and extensive as the infamous tunnels of Cu Chi, 25 miles northwest of Saigon, but nonetheless they caused difficulties for Free World forces in many parts of South Vietnam – officially called the Republic of Vietnam (RVN). While the VC hiding in tunnels were relatively harmless, for the moment anyway, they allowed the

Infantrymen of the 25th Infantry Division sweep though a village in the Iron Triangle east of Cu Chi. The villager, making a point of ignoring the Americans, could well have camouflaged a tunnel entrance after the local VC ducked into it. (25th Infantry Division Museum)

VC to hide and then fight another day. Tunnels also served as hiding places for weapons, ammunition, food, and supplies, and provided command centers, aid stations, hospitals, repair shops, classrooms, and other facilities.

The main problem was that the tunnels rendered search-and-destroy missions ineffective. Once Free World forces had "cleared" an area, the VC emerged from their tunnels and continued their activities. It was also irksome for Free World troops to know that the enemy was hiding just feet away and were unreachable. Efforts were made to detect tunnel entrances and air vents. Explosives might be placed in discovered entrances, but that accomplished little in the more extensive complexes owing to hidden exits allowing escape, air and water locks to dampen blast concussion, angular turns, and other protective measures.

To catch a rat, set a rat, or a ferret. It did little good to learn how to detect tunnel entrances and air vents and collapse entrances, but not to ferret out the enemy. Someone had to go in and get them. That was not the tunnel rats' main objective, however. It was important to learn just how extensive a tunnel complex was; this did not mean that the entire system had to be explored, but at least an idea gleaned as to its extent. This allowed more effective operations to be conducted in the future. More importantly, weapons, munitions, supplies, and documents had to be recovered or destroyed. Efforts were made to destroy tunnels to some degree, thereby preventing their continued use.

When the extent of the tunnels in Vietnam was realized, it was discovered that the Army of the Republic of Vietnam (ARVN) had known of them for some time. However, they had not realized their scale. This is understandable because they had never sent anyone into them, it being considered suicidal. It was also found that while scout dogs could sometimes detect tunnel entrances, they absolutely refused to enter them.

At first, infantrymen volunteered to enter the tunnels: extremely gusty infantrymen armed with only pistols and flashlights. The "tunnel runners" were born. The Australians originally called them "tunnel ferrets." They came to be known simply as "tunnel rats," with the unofficial motto of *Non Gratum Anus Rodentum* – "Not Worth a Rat's Ass." A slogan, indicating the tunnel rats' willingness to help out in a dangerous situation, was, "Don't you fear, the tunnel rats are here."

ABOVE LEFT
An old truck tire in a village junk heap was used to conceal a tunnel entrance. It had had other scrap and debris piled atop it. (25th Infantry Division Museum)

ABOVE
Reconnaissance platoon members (note the tiger-stripe and woodlands camouflage uniforms) of the 25th Infantry Division pass rope down to a tunnel rat. This tunnel is unusual as it was set in a relatively open cultivated field. (25th Infantry Division Museum)

CHRONOLOGY

1945

21 July — Vietnam divided at the 17th Parallel after the French withdraw.

1955

March — First US military advisors arrive in Vietnam.

1959

January — North Vietnam issues resolution that changes its "political struggle" in South Vietnam to an "armed struggle."

May — North Vietnam begins major improvements to the Ho Chi Minh Trail in order to supply its struggle in the south.

1960

December — National Liberation Front (Viet Cong) is formed.

1962

6 February — Military Assistance Command, Vietnam (MACV), formed to control all US armed forces in RVN.

1964

2–4 August — Destroyers USS *Maddox* and USS *C. Turner Joy* are allegedly attacked by North Vietnamese torpedo boats in the Gulf of Tonkin.

7 August — US Congress passes Gulf of Tonkin Resolution to counter North Vietnamese aggression.

1965

7 February — VC attacks US installations in Pleiku. Air attacks on North Vietnam are authorized, which commence on February 24.

8 March — First US Marine ground combat troops arrive in RVN.

6 April — US ground troops are authorized to conduct offensive operations.

7 May — First US Army conventional ground combat troops arrive in RVN (173rd Airborne Brigade).

30 July — US Army, Vietnam (USARV), is formed to control Army forces.

22 August — First US combat engineer battalion (70th) arrives in RVN.

11 September — 1st Cavalry Division (Airmobile) arrives in RVN.

14 September — First Royal Australian Engineers unit (3 Troop, 1 Field Squadron) arrives in RVN.

2 October — 1st Infantry Division arrives in RVN.

8 October	First use of Mity Mite sprayer to fill tunnels with tear gas (5th ARVN Infantry Division).

1966
8–14 January	Operation *Crimp*, the first major effort to clear the Cu Chi area, where extensive tunnel systems were discovered.
8 January	First use of tear-gas barrel bombs dropped from CH-47 helicopters (1st Cavalry Division).
28 March	25th Infantry Division arrives in RVN.
25 September	4th Infantry Division arrives in RVN.
16 December	9th Infantry Division arrives in RVN.

1967
8–26 January	Operation *Cedar Falls*, in which the extent of the Cu Chi tunnels is fully realized.
25 September	Americal Division activated in RVN.
19 November	101st Airborne Division arrives in RVN.

1968
30 January	VC and NVA initiate the Tet Offensive, which ends February 26.
31 March	US Government announces de-escalation of its war effort and halts bombing of North Vietnam.
12 May	Peace talks begin in Paris.

1969
8 June	US initiates Vietnamization program to completely turn the war effort over to RVN forces.

1970
29 April	Offensive operations into Cambodia to neutralize NVA/VC sanctuaries.

1973
15 January	US announces halt to all offensive ground action.
27 January	Ceasefire agreement is signed in Paris, and US conscription ceases.
29 March	Last US troops are withdrawn from RVN and MACV is disbanded.

1975
29 April	The US embassy in Saigon is evacuated.
30 April	Saigon falls to NVA forces.

RECRUITMENT

Tunnel rats were recruited in exactly the same way as other soldiers; their tunnel-exploration activities were in addition to whatever basic military occupation they engaged in day to day. The initial recruitment of tunnel rats is therefore identical to that of "normal" soldiers, which indeed all tunnel rats were. During the Vietnam War, men might have been conscripted for two years or voluntarily enlist for three. It was an unpopular war, but that did not mean that the majority of soldiers, whether drafted or volunteers, had a negative attitude. There were many, including draftees, who gave it their best. The highest demand was for infantrymen. With nine to 11 infantry battalions per division and four in separate brigades, a good many soldiers were assigned as infantrymen regardless of what their preference may have been.

Contrary to popular conception, neither the average soldier nor the majority of soldiers in Vietnam were draftees. Approximately two-thirds were volunteers, though many had probably hoped not to be deployed to Vietnam. Coincidently, two-thirds of the soldiers who served in World War II were draftees. Approximately 70 percent of those killed in action in Vietnam were volunteers. It is often said that the average age of infantrymen in Vietnam was 19. It was actually 22. It would have been higher if the full complement of mid- and senior-grade NCOs were available, but since there were shortages of those grades, the average age of infantrymen was much lower, but not as low as 19. Recruitment and training of infantrymen is addressed in Warrior 98: *US Army Infantryman in Vietnam 1965–73* (Osprey: Oxford, 2005).

As there were no tunnel rat units or standardized practices, tunnel rats were "recruited" in different ways. Often it was simply a call for volunteers on the spot. Tunnels or caves were discovered and they needed to be checked. Some tunnel rats preformed the job only one or two times, as it became necessary. It was simply a matter of who was available and willing. Often there was no intent to explore or plot tunnel routes, but simply to determine if they were occupied and to recover any weapons, munitions, or documents. In most cases, tunnel rats were infantrymen, engineers, cavalry scouts, and chemical specialists, who carried out this dangerous mission in addition to

The camouflage has been stripped from this bunker. Several such bunkers were sometimes linked together by tunnels or simple shallow crawl trenches covered by camouflage. (Tom Laemlein/Armor Plate Press)

This tunnel entrance proves to be a tight fit for a 25th Infantry Division tunnel rat. Helmets were sometimes worn during the initial entry, but often discarded because of the confined space. (25th Infantry Division Museum)

whatever other duties they usually preformed. There were instances when tunnel rats were formed into teams to be available on-call when necessary. These might be assembled into teams in the battalion headquarters company. More often than not, tunnel rat teams were ad hoc groups of two to six men.

The qualities needed to be tunnel rats were evident. The most obvious was that they had to be immune to claustrophobia, but that in itself was not enough. They had to be able to crawl through a narrow tunnel for prolonged periods in absolute darkness, and be unaffected by highly probable encounters with bugs, snakes, rodents, and other vermin, as well as deadly close combat in the worst possible conditions. They had to crawl through mud and flooded tunnels, search for booby traps, deal with choking smoke and tear gas (known as CS), and endure the stench of the dead and of human waste. It is one thing to crawl through a small tunnel in pitch blackness, and another to plunge into a water lock (a portion of flooded tunnel) and trust that it was not too long only because it was assumed that a VC could hold his breath for only a short time as well. All too often it could be a dead end, and it would then be a long way back to the entrance – moving backwards. Tunnel rats may have worn gasmasks to protect them from tear gas, but tear gas also affected moist skin and there was no protection from that. There was also the danger of oxygen starvation. Tunnel rats required acute hearing, something that many troops that had been in combat for even a short time suffered a deficiency in. They had to be able to detect the faintest sounds of movement.

As with any volunteer job in the Army, one could "un-volunteer." One does not of course un-volunteer from combat, but tunnel exploration was obviously a special case. It offered a high possibility of developing severe claustrophobia, which was something that could completely incapacitate a soldier underground. Tunnel rats had to be completely willing and able to undertake the job. Physically, they needed to be of a small stature. The job also required agility, strength, and the ability to perform difficult tasks in cramped confines. This included probing, digging, forcing open trapdoors, disarming booby traps, fastening ropes to material being recovered, and emplacing demolitions.

TRAINING

There was no Military Occupation Specialty (MOS) for tunnel rats. They were mostly combat engineers (12B), infantryman (11B), armored reconnaissance specialists (11D), and chemical-operations specialists (54A). Mortar (11C) and antiarmor (11H) crewmen often found themselves underemployed and pressed as 11B infantrymen. They too were a source of tunnel rats. Both Basic Combat Training (BCT) and Advanced Individual Training (AIT) taught a variety of skills that would be valuable to future tunnel rats. It was also found that having men with different MOSs within a tunnel rat team brought a broad range of experience, which proved very useful in the field.

Basic Combat Training

All US soldiers, from cooks to infantrymen, undertook the eight-week BCT course, regardless of their future MOS. This was preceded by "Zero Week," in which administrative processing, inoculations, testing, and uniform issue was conducted. BCT was conducted at over 20 training centers across the country. The goals of BCT was to instill military discipline and confidence, get recruits in physical shape, learn dismounted drill, learn to live in the field, qualify with the M14 rifle (83 hours of training and firing), live and operate as part of a unit, follow orders, and learn the rudiments of military service and individual combat skills. This included a wide range of subjects: hand-to-hand combat, bayonet fighting, chemical-warfare defense, first aid, guard duty, map reading, and the use of hand grenades.

One experience in BCT of particular benefit to future tunnel rats was the dreaded gas chamber. This was hyped up quite a bit by drill sergeants, with trainees living in fear of the unavoidable event. Soldiers received only four hours of chemical, biological, and radiological (CBR) warfare orientation. This mainly entailed the use of the M17 protective mask, simply called the "gasmask." The M17 was made of a black rubber-like plastic face-piece with large bug-like eyepieces, providing a relatively wide field of vision. Rather than an awkward air-filter canister on the side of the face piece or the snout, low-profile internal filters were fitted on both cheeks. The voice-emitter, allowing verbal communication, was set in the snout. Adjustable web straps allowed the mask to be fitted round the back of the head; it would be worn under the helmet. The mask was carried in a canvas case secured to the soldier's left hip by shoulder and leg straps. It was hot to wear and caused sweating in even mild weather, restricted vision somewhat, and was claustrophobic to wear for some men.

Trainees leaned that when a gas alarm was sounded one had to stop breathing, remove the mask from the case, and don it in a matter of seconds. They were then to clear the mask by slapping their hands over the filters and exhaling sharply. This prevented the exhaled air from being blown through the filters, but blew air and contaminates out from under the face-piece's edges instead. Theoretically, the soldier could now breathe normally, although it was akin to breathing with a towel wrapped over one's face. If running or exerting oneself, it was difficult to draw in enough air.

The M17 mask offered protection from chemical-warfare agents (nerve, choking, blistering, blood, and irritant agents), most biological agents, and radioactive contaminates. What it did not protect from was oxygen starvation. This meant that a large volume of smoke (including that from smoke grenades) and tear gas in a confined space could suffocate a person,

as smoke and tear gas displace oxygen. This would require an extremely concentrated volume of smoke or tear gas for a prolonged period.

The gas chamber was simply a small cinderblock building with two airtight rooms set in a remote training area. It had steel entry and exit doors on opposite ends and no windows. The trainees were motivated with war chants and a great deal of yelling to build up courage. They entered one room wearing their masks. The room was filled with diluted chlorine gas. Even if inhaled, the worst that could happen was a mild headache. The trainees believed the gas was lethal. They stood against the walls of the chamber and were instructed to take three deep breaths to fill their lungs with oxygen. When given the order, they lifted their masks off their faces, continuing to hold their breath. Even though they were holding their breath, they could smell a scent like laundry bleach. When tapped by the instructor, they would replace their masks and clear them by blowing residual gas out the sides. They then filed out. The purpose was to provide self-confidence and confidence in the use of the mask.

The tear-gas chamber was a different matter. Tear-gas pellets were placed in a can in the chamber's center and burned with a heat tablet to fill the room with vapor. Trainees with masks donned ran into the tear-gas-filled room and lined up against the walls. On order, they removed their masks and were told to breathe it in. The effects were immediate, with tears, coughing, gagging, and free-flowing mucus and saliva. The mask-wearing drill sergeants ordered each man to recite his name, rank, service number, and date of birth, or sometimes to sing a song. This ensured that they remained in the chamber sufficiently long to experience the effects. They were not told to re-don their

Infantrymen wearing M17 protective masks. The radio operator with his sleeves rolled up appears to be feeling the effects of the micro-pulverized CS burning his armpits. Note the coiled sling ropes on the two un-masked men. (Tom Laemlein/Armor Plate Press)

masks, but to place their left hand on the shoulder of the man in front and follow him out when ordered. Clearing the mask in the normal manner would do nothing for the CS powder, which was already in the eyes, nose and mouth; it would only make it worse. Drill instructors watched trainees closely for any adverse reaction and medics were on-hand with oxygen.

Tear-gas use and effects

What is known as CS-1 riot-control agent is also commonly called "tear gas." "CS" is merely a code identifier and not an abbreviation. It is also described as an irritant agent and an incapacitating agent. CS replaced CN (chloracetophenone) in the early 1960s. It is odorless, but there is a faint burnt smell from burning-type CS munitions.

It was one of the tunnel rats' main tools. It causes extreme irritation to the eyes, nose, throat, and lungs. The eyes burn severely and extensive tear flow results. It is virtually impossible to keep the eyes open other than for a few blinking moments; some individuals are unable to open their eyes at all. The need to rub the eyes is impossible to avoid and only increases the burning sensation. The effects are accompanied by excessive mucus flow from the nose and saliva from the mouth. Moist skin areas, especially the underarms and groin, itch and burn. Sunburned areas are also affected. Rubbing exposed skin areas only rubs in the CS powder. In extreme and prolonged instances of inhaling CS causes respiratory problems. Many Vietnamese thought tear gas would cause some form of illness, but could not say what that illness or its symptoms were. Individuals experiencing CS for the first time can easily panic, especially if in a dark confined space. This is another reason why US soldiers were exposed to CS in training, to give them the experience and confidence to cope with it.

The "gas" is actually an ultra microfine powder and not a gas. The powder can settle on the ground and vegetation and when disturbed will rise up and affect anyone in the area. Particles will also cling to tunnel walls. It usually loses its potency within six days, but can last longer in dry weather.

Powdered CS was dispersed by dropping 55-gallon drums from helicopters, attached to explosives and detonated inside tunnels, or dispersed by Mity Mite blowers into tunnels. Limited use was made of 105mm howitzer XM629, 4.2in. mortar XM630, and 40mm grenade-launcher XM651 CS projectiles.

A straightforward description of the experience provides a trainee's view of the effects of CS:

Pulling the mask up when ordered, you first smell a burnt dusty odor. We of course held our breath as long as possible and kept our eyes shut. Since we had to shout our name, rank, and number, it was unavoidable. In seconds I felt my eyes burning and I could feel burning in my nose and mouth. It got worse in seconds and some guys tried to run for the door with sergeants grabbing them and ordering them to freeze. Most stuck it out. In a few more seconds my eyes were burning so bad that it took everything I had to not rub them. Snot started running from my nose like I've never seen and I was drooling saliva like a dog on a hot day. Everything burned, even my armpits. Everyone was bending over coughing and gagging, spitting and yelling at the top of their lungs. I couldn't see a thing and my eyes were burning and stinging like mad. No one panicked, but when they said, "get out of here," there was no hesitation. Everyone kept their arm on the man in front and a sergeant led us out. Everyone rushed away from the building and faced into the wind as we'd been told. We started washing our eyes with canteens and they had more water for us. The sergeants were checking on everyone and asking if we were okay, as well as keeping us from running into trees. It was only a few minutes before we got over it and then everyone was laughing, joking, and talking. I remember a sergeant telling us not to wear these fatigues again until they were washed. It was bad and a little scary, but we felt like we had done something difficult and most were proud of it.

Graduation from BCT was a milestone regardless of whether trainees had considered it a good, bad, or indifferent experience. A "cycle book" filled with photos of their comrades and training events was given to each man. They were now soldiers, but they still had their MOS training to accomplish. Usually trainees undertook BCT at the same post they would undertake infantry AIT (this stands for "Advanced Individual Training," not "Advanced Infantry Training" as is sometimes reported). However, it was not uncommon for them to take BCT at one post and then be transferred to another post to undertake infantry AIT or another MOS.

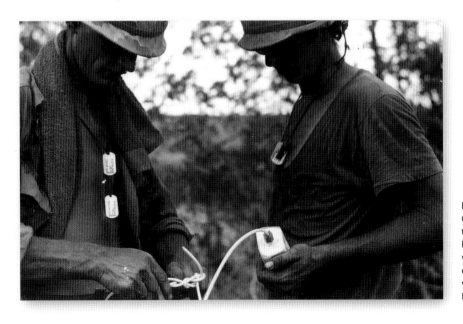

Engineers prepare 2½lb M5A1 C4 demolition charges and link them to detcord with half-hitch knots. The man to the right is wearing his helmet camouflage cover with the brown side out, which is unusual. (1st Cavalry Division Museum)

The replica VC village at Tigerland, Fort Polk, Louisiana. Clockwise from upper left: The village's flooded defensive moat with blunt punji stakes; the interior of a thatch hooch; the intersection of the three corrugated steel-lined tunnels with a hidden entrance above and on each end; a trapdoor hidden beneath a table. (Fort Polk Museum)

Infantry Advanced Individual Training

This was where soldiers learned the skills of their job, and were awarded an MOS. Training for the three infantry MOSs – 11B (light infantryman), 11C (indirect-fire [mortar] crewman), and 11H (antiarmor [recoilless rifle] crewman) – was conducted at Fort Campbell, Kentucky; Fort Dix, New Jersey; Fort Gordon, Georgia; Fort McClellan, Alabama; Fort Ord, California; and Fort Polk, Louisiana. Combat engineer training was undertaken at Fort Leonard Wood, Missouri, and chemical-warfare specialists were trained at Fort McClellan, Alabama. Armored cavalry scouts were trained at Fort Knox, Kentucky, at the Armor School.

Infantry training took eight weeks and included individual tactical skills, combat and reconnaissance patrolling, squad and platoon offensive and defensive tactics, live-fire tactical exercises, and qualification with the M14A1 automatic rifle, M60 machine gun, and .45-cal. pistol. There was also familiarization firing of the 40mm M79 grenade launcher, 90mm M67 recoilless rifle, 3.5in. M20A1B1 rocket launcher (bazooka), and the M72 LAW. A brief amount of training time was spent on the laying, detecting, and removal of landmines as well as detecting and setting booby traps. This was accomplished using US firing devices and explosive items, with little orientation on the many and varied VC/NVA booby traps. Tunnel rats encountered many traps and explosives in tunnels, and so this training was especially valuable for them.

Most infantry AIT training centers were rated "Vietnam-oriented." The exception was Fort Dix, which trained personnel destined for assignments other than Vietnam. "Vietnam-oriented" meant that a small Vietnamese village was erected, sometimes with adjacent replica rice paddies. One was even built at Fort Dix even though it was not a Vietnam-oriented training center.

Trainees conducted an exercise where they cordoned off the village and searched it. Various simple booby traps, hiding places, and defenses and perimeter obstacles were found in these villages, including perimeter berms and ditches filled with fake punji stakes. Trainees found it humorous when conducting simulated assaults on a "Vietnamese" village in the winter months as they slid across frozen rice paddies. Some centers went so far as to provide a simple tunnel system.

The author experienced the replicated Vietnamese village's tunnel system at Peason Ridge Training Area north of Fort Polk, Louisiana, in 1967. Other than being underground, it bore little resemblance to actual VC tunnel systems. It had a Y-shaped layout and was less than 100ft long, with three unimaginatively hidden entrances inside hooches. It was about 5ft below ground and had no air vents, water or air locks, sharp angular turns, hidden passages, side rooms, or any of the facilities and amenities found in actual complexes. It was lined with 4ft-diameter corrugated steel culvert pipe, which was much more spacious the 2½ft-wide and 3–4ft-high or smaller tunnels typically found in Vietnam. Another problem was that the steel-lined tunnels prevented troops from practicing plotting the route using a magnetic compass. The area's high water table ensured that it partially flooded after rains.

Other than a day or two in the Vietnamese village there was little actual Vietnam-orientated training except for some additional ambush and counter-ambush exercises. However, basic conventional tactics provided the basis of small-unit tactics in Vietnam, which were modified for the non-linear tropical battlefield (see Elite 186: *Vietnam Infantry Tactics*, Osprey: Oxford, 2011).

Combat engineer Advanced Individual Training

Tunnel rats used explosives extensively to collapse tunnel entrances and destroy caches of enemy equipment, and so combat engineer training was especially valuable. The eight-week-long combat engineer AIT was conducted at Fort Leonard Wood, Missouri. It was better known at "Fort Lost in the Woods Misery" or "Little Korea" in reference to the harsh winters of that country. The training covered many of the same subjects as that for infantry (engineers had a secondary role as infantry and had to be able to defend their worksites), but with less emphasis on tactics and live-fire exercises. Engineer training concentrated on land navigation, map reading, rigging (working with ropes and block and tackle), knot-tying, the use of hand and power tools,

Combat engineers learned a great many skills during AIT at Fort Leonard Wood, Missouri, many of which proved useful to tunnel rats. Here trainees learn how to rig a block and tackle. (US Army)

Among the many jobs assigned to engineers in Vietnam, an important one was clearing vegetation in order to create firebases, fields of fire, and helicopter landing and pickup zones. Besides demolitions materials and bulldozers, machetes and chainsaws were used. Chainsaws were also useful for clearing vegetation and manmade structures from around tunnel entrances. (Tom Laemlein/Armor Plate Press)

the use of the pneumatic jackhammer, the laying of steel matting for airstrips and roads, constructing timber bridges, erecting panel and floating bridges, small-boat handling, constructing poncho rafts, constructing barbed-wire obstacles and field fortifications, camouflage, mine laying and clearance, and

ENGINEER DEMOLITIONS TRAINING

The staff sergeant here has prepared a display of demolition materials most commonly used in Vietnam. He wears the stateside fatigue uniform with combat boots and a white-painted helmet liner and instructor armband ("INSTR") identifying him as being on the Demolition Committee. Training centers wore the shoulder insignia of the army area in which they were located, which in this example is Fifth Army. In July 1966 the name and US Army tapes were ordered changed to black on olive drab, but it took almost two years for the changeover to take place.

The ¼lb TNT charge (**1**) was mainly used for training and was not commonly employed in combat. The ½lb TNT charge (**2**) was less widely used than the 1lb TNT charge (**3**), which was widely used, but in general C4 saw much more use than TNT, especially since TNT produced dangerous fumes underground. The TNT charges were contained in water-resistant fiberboard covers with metal end caps and a cap well in one end. The 2½lb M5A1 C4 demolition block (**4**) had clear plastic covers and white plastic ends with cap wells in both. M5A1 blocks were replaced by the M112, but remaining stocks were expended in Vietnam. The 1¼lb (500g) M112 C4 demolition charge (**5**) was covered in Mylar with an adhesive backing, and was by far the most frequently used charge in the field. The M118 C4 demolition charge (**6**) held four ½lb, ½in.-thick sheet charges. The M183 demolition-charge assembly (**7**) held 16 M112 charges and four priming assemblies (5ft of detcord with an RDX booster on each end) in an M183 haversack. They could be used as individual charges or as a satchel charge. Detcord (**8**) was used to link together demolition charges for simultaneous detonation; it was not a timed safety fuse. The 15lb M2A3 shaped-charge (**9**) held 11½lb of Composition A3. It was contained in a fiberboard casing with a 6in. base that attached to the lower end, providing standoff from the target. It could penetrate 36in. of reinforced concrete. The 40lb M3 shaped charge (**10**) with detachable 15in legs could punch through 60in. of concrete. The ammonium-nitrate 40lb cratering charge (**11**) contained 40lb of Composition H6 and was used to blast large craters in roads and to blow apart obstacles. It proved very useful for destroying tunnels. Earlier ammonium-nitrate-filled charges were also used. The M1A2 bangalore torpedo (**12**) was 5ft long and contained 10½lb of Composition B4. Used for breaching wire obstacles and minefields, they could be attached end-to-end up to a total length of 200ft. In Vietnam they were used to blast paths through dense bamboo thickets. Most of the charges shown here are still in use today.

operating AN/PRS-3 mine detectors. Many of these skills would prove invaluable to tunnel rats. Almost a week was spent on demolitions training, learning about all the different explosives, materials, and equipment, including electric and non-electric firing systems, and how to calculate and emplace charges on different types of targets. Weapons training included the M79 grenade launcher, M60 machine gun, 3.5in. bazooka, and M72 LAW.

APPEARANCE

There were no height or weight requirements for infantrymen and engineers, although they were required to be in first-rate physical condition: what was known as a "picket-fence profile," that is, "111111." The PULHES profile included: P – Physical capacity or stamina, U – Upper extremities, L – Lower extremities, H – Hearing and ears, E – Eyes, and S – Psychiatric. A "2" or "3" in any of these six categories disqualified an individual from the combat arms (infantry, armor, combat engineers, and artillery). An exception was a "2" in hearing for artillerymen, the reasoning being that they would eventually damage their hearing anyway.

Most tunnel rats were of small stature. The average Vietnamese male was 5ft 1in. to 5ft 4in. tall, and weighed 110–122lb. The average American soldier was 5ft 8in. tall and weighed 120–180lb; he would have a difficult time navigating tunnels custom built for Vietnamese men. Obviously, smaller-statured Americans made better tunnel rats, but larger-framed tunnel rats were not unknown. Regardless of height, they needed to be limber.

Into the ground

There was no prescribed tunnel rat "uniform." Before descending into the abyss the tunnel rat prepared for the job by removing all of his web gear and some of his "surface uniform." The jungle fatigue uniform consisted of the commonly worn pants and shirt. Many tunnel rats removed their shirt, as its cargo pockets and loose sleeves could easily snag on obstructions. If the shirt was retained, the sleeves were usually worn down to protect the elbows when crawling, as they snagged less than rolled-up sleeves. Some men tucked their shirt into their pants. Those removing their shirts may have worn their undershirt while others went bare-chested. Many men did not wear undershirts or even underwear, owning to sweat retention,

A tunnel rat prepares to enter a tunnel. Note the olive-drab towel used as a "drive-on rag" around the neck to mop up sweat and clean off mud and dirt. (25th Infantry Division Museum)

which resulted in rashes and chaffing, especially in the groin and underarm areas. Such rashes were uncomfortable and could become infected. Occasionally men reduced the naturally baggy jungle-fatigue pants by securing the lower legs with "550 cord," web straps, or green duct tape.

The tight confines of a Hobo Woods tunnel are demonstrated here by a 25th Infantry Division tunnel rat equipped with his two most common and valuable tools, an MX-199/U flashlight and a .45-cal. Colt M1911A1 pistol. (Tom Laemlein/Armor Plate Press)

ABOVE
Infantrymen lower a tunnel rat into an entrance shaft. The VC probably used a bamboo ladder, which may have been taken into the tunnel with them. (25th Infantry Division Museum)

ABOVE RIGHT
A 1st Cavalry Division volunteer discards his M16A1 rifle and helmet. He wears an M17 protective mask case on his left hip. This tunnel entrance is hidden in a pig pen, something that a soldier would be reluctant to search. (Tom Laemlein/Armor Plate Press)

An issue olive-drab towel or a triangular bandage was often worn by soldiers in the field to mop up sweat. Tunnel rats found it useful to wipe sweat and dust off their faces or clean mud off their hands to allow them to do delicate work. Wristwatches, dog tags, and rings were removed to prevent snagging. They carried grenade arming pins to deactivate booby-trapped grenades. US grenade pins would fit into Soviet and Chinese grenades.

Most tunnel rats went in bareheaded so as to have unrestricted vision and hearing. It meant that one could expect some bumps on the head, but clear vision and hearing were essential. Some occasionally wore steel helmets and others just the helmet liner as a lighter alternative. Hair was generally worn short for hygienic reasons in the hot and humid climate, but longish hair was not unknown. Kneepads and/or gloves may have been worn. Jungle boots were typically worn with the pants bloused into them. On rare instances tennis shoes were worn. It was common to douse oneself with insect repellent before entering a tunnel in order to ward off leeches, mosquitoes, spiders, scorpions, fleas, ants, and other creepy crawlies.

 COMBAT ENGINEER

Combat engineers appeared little different from infantrymen. This engineer, undertaking a light construction project, wears the M1 steel helmet (with grenade-arming pins in the camouflage band, for neutralizing booby traps) and the M1952 body-armor vest. He has removed his jungle fatigue shirt, owing to the heat. He is outfitted with basic M1956 web gear with two ammunition pouches holding two 20-round magazines each; infantrymen typically carried more. An M61 fragmentation grenade is hooked on his vest. This was the same as the M26A1, but had a wire safety clip securing the arming lever. Called a "jungle clip," it prevented the grenade from arming if the pin was snagged on vegetation. He is armed with an M14 rifle, but engineer units received M16A1 rifles soon after the infantry did. He carries a D-handle shovel, an essential tool of war for a combat engineer. Other gear includes a 3-gallon canvas bucket (**1**), work gloves (**2**), M1938 wire cutters (**3**), an 18in. machete with plastic scabbards (**4**), and a 500ft roll of engineer tape (**5**). This was a 2in.-wide white, non-adhesive tape used to mark lanes through minefields. It saw practical application when used to mark tent guy lines, barbed wire, open holes, and anything else a soldier could trip on in firebases at night. Short strips would be tied to vegetation to mark discovered tunnel entrances, air vents, mines, and booby traps. He also carries a stainless-steel utility pocketknife, commonly called a "demo knife" (**6**). It had a 3in. knife blade, a screwdriver/bottle cap-lifter, a can opener, and an awl (punch). The M2 cap crimper (**7**) (also known as a "fuse crimper"), besides crimping blasting caps on time fuse and detcord, provided a screwdriver, a punch for making blasting cap holes in C4, and a fuse and detcord cutter. One of many variants of unofficial Tunnel Rat patches is shown at (**8**). It depicted a flashlight-and-pistol-armed rat and was inscribed *Non Gratum Anus Rodentum* (Not Worth A Rat's Ass).

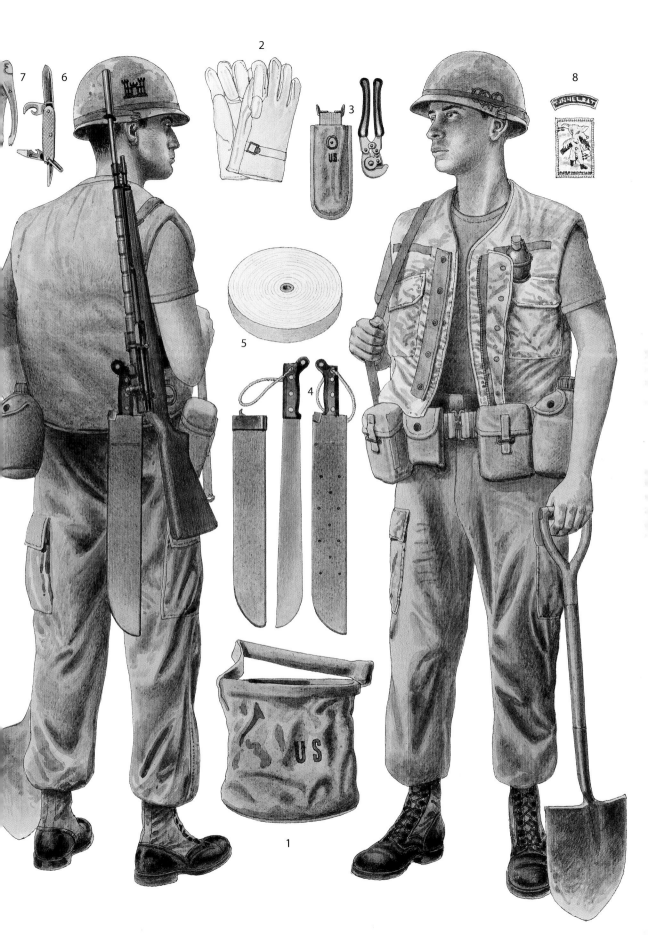

EQUIPMENT AND WEAPONS

Tunnel rats needed light and compact weapons, preferably with a sound suppressor. A single gunshot in a tunnel's confinement was excruciatingly loud and damaged one's hearing. Firing a .45-cal. pistol inside a tight-fitting tunnel was deafeningly painful and caused permanent hearing damage. It literally feels like nails are driven into one's ears. They were used only as a last resort. Few suppressed weapons were available, and standard handguns were commonly used. Hearing protection could be worn, but it was essential for tunnel rats to be able to hear the faintest sounds of movement in the pitch-black tunnels, so they typically went without. Most items of equipment used for tunnel exploration and destruction were readily available standard-issue items, though sometimes used in a manner different than that for which they were originally intended.

Tunnel rat weapons

The standard weapons carried by most infantrymen were unsuitable for use in the extremely confined spaces where tunnel rats could expect to fight, being much too large to use conveniently, if at all. As tunnel rats usually carried a flashlight with them into tunnel complexes, it was important to be able to use something that could be aimed and fired with one hand. For these reasons, handguns were the weapons of choice.

The most common of these was the standard-issue Colt .45-cal. M1911A1 pistol with a seven-round magazine. They were readily available, with almost 30 in a rifle company and at least a dozen in an engineer company. Some use was made of Smith & Wesson Model 10 and Colt Police Positive Special revolvers, which were normally issued to aviators. Both held six relatively underpowered .38-cal. Special rounds. They made almost as loud a report as the .45-cal. Some use was made of privately purchased .38-cal. Special and .357-cal. Magnum revolvers and .45-cal. ACP and 9mm pistols of various makes. Occasionally, .30-cal. M2 carbines with the barrel cut back to the forearm and the butt stock sawn off leaving a pistol grip were used.

Hi-Standard .22-cal. Long Rifle Model HD semi-automatic pistols with a 10-round magazines were occasionally issued. Sometimes the Model HDM with a non-removable silencer was provided – originally acquired by the Office of Strategic Services (OSS) in 1943. The silencer had a life of about 200 rounds, which was not a serious drawback as they were so seldom fired. Another .22-cal. Long Rifle semi-automatic seeing some use was the Ruger Mk I Target pistol, which also used a 10-round magazine. These had originally been used as training and match pistols. A .22-cal. firearm is not a potent weapon, but at ranges of a few feet and with repeated rapid shots, it did the job.

In 1966 the Army issued six experimental tunnel-exploration kits. With the kits came an S&W .38-cal. Special Model 10 revolver with a silencer and aiming light. The aiming light was unnecessary and the silencer too long, making the weapon unbalanced. Silencers do not really work on revolvers, owning to the slight gap between the cylinder and the rear end of the barrel, but they

An automatic rifleman armed with a 7.62mm M14(M) automatic rifle fitted with an M6 bayonet coaxes a VC out of a tunnel. Mats and corrugated tin had been used to cover the hole. (Tom Laemlein/Armor Plate Press)

The angular entrance to a tunnel has been cleared and a tunnel rat prepares to enter. This 1st Infantry Division tunnel rat appears to be armed with a .40-cal. Quiet Special Purpose Revolver based on the S&W Model 29. He wears a shoulder holster rig and holds a pen flashlight in his left hand. (Tom Laemlein/Armor Plate Press)

did greatly reduce the sharp report and ear damage. Another problem was that the silencer was designed to be used with half-load rounds, but only full-load M41 rounds were available in Vietnam.

A total of 75 specially modified S&W Model 29 revolvers were issued in 1969. They fired a special .40-cal. shot cartridge designed to make a report no louder than a .22-cal. Long Rifle. The shot cartridges held 15 7.5-grain tungsten steel pellets in a plastic sabot (a .117-cal. BB weighs 5–6 grains) and used the gas seal piston concept to reduce its noise signature. The revolvers were designated the Quiet Special Purpose Revolver (QSPR), also known as "tunnel revolvers" or "tunnel guns." It had no sights, and had a 1.37in.-long (35mm) smoothbore barrel with a 30ft range. These revolvers were inexplicitly withdrawn after six months, probably because they performed poorly owing to the unusual cartridge system, which may not have been sufficiently lethal. Even its reduced report was too loud in a tunnel's confines.

Hand grenades included M26 "lemon" and M67 "baseball" fragmentation grenades, Mk 3A2 "demolition or concussion" grenades, and M34 white phosphorus ("Willie Pete") grenades. Blast and fragmentation grenades could not be used underground. Even tossing a grenade around a 90-degree tunnel bend would create far too much blast over-pressure in the confined space. They were routinely thrown into tunnel entrances to clear a portion of the tunnel up to the first bend, making it deadly for any VC personnel to remain anywhere close to entrances. The concussion grenade, containing 8oz of TNT, was particularly effective for this compared to the M67 fragmentation grenade, which contained 6.5oz of Composition B. With a fiber body, the Mk 3 generated little fragmentation. M18 colored- (red, yellow, violet, or green) and AN-M8 white-smoke grenades were widely used, along with M7A2

Debris is shoveled away from a tunnel entrance after a shattering explosive detonation that virtually disintegrated the surrounding vegetation. (25th Infantry Division Museum)

A 1st Infantry Division soldier in the Iron Triangle peers into a partly hidden bunker entrance with an M2A1-7 portable flamethrower. Flamethrowers were little used in Vietnam owing to their 70lb weight when full, and the fact that they were expended in seconds. They would then have to be refueled and repressurized using equipment that could not be man-packed through the jungle. (Tom Laemlein/Armor Plate Press)

CS grenades

The ABC-M7A2 and ABC-M7A3 riot-control hand grenades, commonly known as "CS" or "tear-gas" grenades, were important tools in tunnel warfare. These beer-can-sized grenades began spewing tear gas within two seconds after releasing the arming lever. The M7A2 was filled with 3.5oz of CS in gelatin capsules with 5.5oz of burning mixture. The M7A3 had 4.5oz of pelletized CS with 7.45oz of burning mixture. There were four holes in the grenade's top and one in the bottom, through which burning CS escaped. They burned for 15–35 seconds, but for 20 seconds on average. When ignited, the grenade grew extremely hot and would burn one's hands if picked up; it would remain hot for some time. The M7A2 grenade weighed 14oz and the M7A3 weighed 15.5oz. The M54 CS grenade adopted in the late 1960s was an M7A3 with an 8–12-second M226 delay fuse for dropping from helicopters.

Another type of riot-control grenade was the ABC-M25A2. This was an 8oz baseball-shaped bursting-type grenade with a plastic body. It was activated by pulling the C12 igniter's arming pin while retaining a spring-loaded sleeve over the top of the fuse with the thumb. When thrown, the small button-like sleeve flew off and the grenade burst in 1.4–3 seconds, spreading a 5m cloud of CS. The CS was mixed with silica aerogel to more effectively spread the tear gas. Being spherical and lighter, it could easily be chucked down a tunnel's length.

and M7A3 riot-control grenades (see sidebar). Thermite-filled AN-M14 incendiary grenades were used to destroy enemy equipment such as heavy weapons and radios. They burned at 4,330°F and could melt through steel.

The M1A1 white-smoke pot weighed 12lb and was contained in a 5.5in-diameter, 8in.-high can. It had a screw-on cap with a 10-second delay friction igniter. It produced gray-white smoke for five to eight minutes. This could be pumped into tunnels via a Mity Mite blower to smoke out the occupants. Less used was the 30lb ABC-M5 white-smoke pot.

Tunnel rat equipment

Engineers and infantrymen carried much the same field equipment, which was made up of a rucksack and load-bearing equipment (LBE), known as "web gear." Generally this consisted of a pistol belt, suspenders, two or more ammunition pouches, one or two canteens, a first-aid pouch, and other gear. Out of necessity, the tunnel rat could carry only what was absolutely necessary. The less encumbered he was, the better he could do his job. In tight spaces he needed to take up as little space as possible, and unnecessary equipment would only get in the way, especially when he had to be a contortionist.

Tunnel teams assembled kits with the necessary equipment, to which they added and removed items as experience dictated. The gear might be carried in large wooden ammunition crates, duffle bags, or aviators' kit bags. A "light" tunnel-exploration kit might consist of the following:

- Protective masks (x2)
- TA-1/PT field telephones (x2)
- MX-306 telephone wire spool
- Lensatic compasses (x2)
- Sealed beam 12-volt flashlights (x2)
- .22-cal. HD or Mk I pistols (x2)
- Probing rods (12in. and 36in.)
- Bayonets (x2)
- Entrenching tool
- Powdered CS (as required in cans)
- M7A2 CS grenades (x12)
- M18 colored-smoke grenades (x4)
- Insect repellent (x4 cans/bottles)

A "heavy" tunnel-exploration kit would contain more bulky equipment and would be employed by tunnel rats expecting to remain underground for extended periods. Some of these items might be:

- Protective masks (x2)
- Body-armor vests (x2)
- 100ft nylon rope
- Grappling hooks (x2)
- TA-1/PT field telephones (x2)
- MX-306 telephone wire spool
- Work gloves (x2 pairs)
- Kneepads (x2 pairs)
- Earplugs (x2 pairs)
- Flashlights (x6) and spare batteries

A combat engineer attaching 2½lb M5A1 C4 demolition charges to trees in order to blast clear a landing zone. The clear plastic-covered charges are linked by detcord. (1st Cavalry Division Museum)

Flashlights were essential, and the wise tunnel rat would carry a spare, but this was not always done. The main model was the MX-991/U right-angle flashlight. It had an olive-drab plastic waterproof body holding two BA-30 batteries. The switch was protected by a guard to prevent the operator accidentally turning it on or off by bumping against something (early models lacked switch guards). There was a clip on the side for attachment to web gear or a belt, and a carrying ring on the bottom. It had a separate compartment in the battery cap, which contained a spare blub and colored filters (red, green, and a diffused white). The red filter helped preserve night vision. This was unnecessary in the tunnels because when the flashlight was extinguished it was absolutely black; one had no night vision as there was no ambient light, just total blackness. For this same reason, "starlight-scope" light-intensification sights were useless as they required ambient light to operate. There was a less-frequently used straight flashlight of similar design, the MX-993/U.

Some use was made of the MX-290/GV lantern. It had a large floodlight on its front and a narrow beam dome light on top. It used a BA-200/U battery and contained spare blubs for both lights. The dome light was protected by a guard and there was a carrying handle. The small aviator's flashlight and other "penlights" were also used.

A miner's headlamp was provided with the experimental tunnel-exploration kits in 1966. It consisted of a six-volt battery-powered headlamp fitted to the front of the field cap ("baseball cap") and was provided with a bite-operated on and off switch. There were problems with this flashlight, including a poorly functioning bite switch, the front-heavy cap being pulled forward by the headlamp and by rubbing against low ceilings, and the fact that the cap's visor interfered with vision.

Compasses were used to plot routes through tunnels, and azimuth (direction) changes to be telephoned back to the surface. Usually the backup man following the lead tunnel rat handled the compass and telephone, but sometimes the lead man did. The lensatic compass was a standard-issue, fold-open type. The small Waltham wrist compass had a nylon strap, allowing hands-free use. Both compasses had glow-in-the-dark compass points and needles. Neither was waterproof.

Measuring tapes were sometimes used, but was difficult to use in the confined tunnels. Distances were simply estimated and then adjusted on the plot map when additional air vents and entrances were found. The distances between turns were usually only 1–10m, making it easy to estimate the distance by sight alone.

The flashlight and lensatic compass, and sometimes pistols, might be dummy-corded to the user by "550 cord" (parachute suspension line) or old bootlaces. Care had to be taken to prevent dummy cords from snagging on obstructions or becoming entangling with body parts. They were a hindrance in a hand-to-hand fight, giving the opponent something else to grab on to.

A vitally important tool for a tunnel rat was his knife. It was used as a probe to aid in detecting hidden doors and buried objects, and as a prying tool to open trapdoors. And of course, it might be needed as a close-combat weapon. The 6.5in. double-edged M6 and M7 knife bayonets for the M14

Each infantry brigade had an attached scout-dog detachment. They were invaluable for sniffing out tunnel entrances. There was no way a dog could be induced to enter a tunnel though. (1st Cavalry Division Museum)

and M16A1 rifles, respectively, were widely used. Air Force survival knives with 5in. blades, and M3 and Ka-Bar Mk 2 fighting knifes, were also popular.

The standard-issue "utility pocketknife" was a Camillus Model 1760 (also made by other manufacturers) commonly called the "demo knife." It was rumored to be made of non-ferrous or non-magnetic metal, making it safe for demolitions work. This is not true, as the blade was made entirely of stainless steel. The TL-29 lineman's pocketknife saw some use. The M2 cap crimper (or "fuse crimper") was made of non-sparking metal, and besides the crimper for attaching blasting caps to time fuse or detcord, it had a screwdriver on one handle, a spike-punch for making cap wells in C4, and a fuse/detcord cutter as the base of the jaws. Steel probing rods of 1–3ft in length were sometimes used, as well as sharpened sticks.

Entrenching tools were used to uncover tunnel entrances and vents, remove camouflage, and widen tunnel entrances. The "tool, entrenching, combination, M1951" was a wooden-handled folding e-tool. It could be locked in a 90-degree angle position to use as a pick or hoe. From about 1969 the all-metal alloy, three-way folding e-tool, the "tool, entrenching, collapsible, M1967," was available. It was a "tri-fold" e-tool with a two-section handle. Tunnel rats also used machetes, which were very useful for clearing camouflage from tunnel entrances. It had an 18in. single-edge blade and was carried in a semi-rigid plastic olive-drab sheath.

Olive-drab nylon rope had a diameter of 7/16in. and was made up of three twisted strands. It came in 120ft rolls or 300ft spools. Small three- and four-prong grappling hooks, sometimes fabricated by a unit welder, were used. These ropes, with or without hooks, were used to drag out equipment and bodies. It was seldom that a tunnel rat would tie a rope to himself to allow him to be pulled out if wounded or killed, as it restricted movement too much. Engineer tape was meant to mark minefields and cleared lanes through them. It was also used to mark tunnel entrances, and was placed around booby traps. It was 2in. wide, white in color, and made of non-adhesive tape. It was issued in 500ft rolls.

Kneepads were used by some tunnel rats, but others found them to be cumbersome. In addition, they were not always available. Expedient kneepads were made by tying field dressings onto the knees by their securing ties. Tan leather gloves were valuable, but they too were not always worn as they were hot and made it difficult to handle weapons. Similar style, but lighter, black leather service gloves were also used. Sometimes the fingertips were cut off. This still protected the hands, but allowed the wearer greater dexterity when using his hands. In wet, muddy tunnels, gloves became very cumbersome, as sticky mud would cling to them. Earplugs were essential when weapons were fired, but tunnel rats could not afford to wear them, as they had to listen for the slightest sounds. Nevertheless, some did when gunplay was expected soon after entering a tunnel. If they were unavailable then some tunnel rats simply tore off cigarette filters and plugged them into their ears.

Small XM28 protective masks were widely used from 1967. They protected only against CS gas, with a warning to that effect marked on the carrying case. While provided with a nylon case, it could be carried in a pants' cargo pocket. The M17 protective mask was designed to protect against most forms of chemical agents. The earlier M9 gas mask with a canister on the left side (some were on the right) saw limited use early in the Vietnam War. These "gas masks" did not protect against oxygen-displacing smoke or flumes. That required a personal air supply, and such equipment was not available, regardless of which is was too heavy and bulky for use by tunnel rats.

For communications, especially when exploring a large tunnel complex, the backup tunnel rat usually carried a TA-1/PT sound-powered field telephone. It required no batteries and was connected to another TA-1/PT or a bulkier, heavier TA-312/PT field telephone on the surface. Two-strand WD-1 field wire was used, dispensed from a MX-306A/G "donut spool" containing half a mile of wire.

Regardless of all the specialized equipment available, photographic evidence shows that most tunnel rats went under the ground equipped only

TUNNEL-EXPLORATION KIT

Units assembled tunnel-exploration kits themselves, and no two were alike. There was a scramble to collect the necessary equipment when a tunnel system was discovered, and they often had to make do with whatever was available. There were some widely used items, especially handguns. The most readily available and commonly used were the Colt .45-cal. M1911A1 pistol (**1**), and the Hi-Standard .22-cal. Model HD pistol (**2**). Above it is the HDM model's fixed silencer (**3**). The Ruger .22-cal. Mk I pistol (**4**) was less commonly used than the Hi-Standard. The S&W .38-cal. Special Model 10 tunnel-exploration revolver (**5**) is shown with a removable silencer and aiming light. Unmodified Model 10s as used by aviators were also used. The .40-cal. smoothbore Quiet Special Purpose Revolver (QSPR) (**6**) was based on the S&W Model 29. The cartridge fired 15 pellets. Only a small number were available, and they were used from April 1969 to 1971. The lightweight and compact XM29 protective mask (**7**) protected the wearer from tear gas only, was introduced in 1968. The bulkier M17 protective mask saw much use (**8**), even after the XM28 was introduced. The TA-1/PT sound-powered field telephone (**9**) was sometimes taken into tunnels to relay route-plotting information and what was discovered. It would be connected to another on the surface via WD-1 wire dispensed from a ½-mile-long MX-306A/G spool (known as a "donut reel") (**10**). The lensatic compass (**11**) was used to determine the tunnel's changes in direction. The MX-991/U right-angle flashlight (**12**) was the most commonly used flashlight, as it could be shone around angles without danger to the tunnel rat. Use was also made of the MX-290/GV six-volt lantern (**13**).

4

5

6

1

3

2

11

12

FOR USE IN RIOT CONTROL AGENTS ONLY

7

8

13

PAYOUT END

MX-306 A/G
KZ 6145-160-7795
DSA 5-25345
UTHWIRE CO

10

9

with a flashlight and .45-cal. automatic, usually barrowed from a grenadier or machine gunner, and wearing only boots, trousers, and an undershirt.

To pump CS through extremely large complexes something more powerful than the Mity Mite blower was necessary. In 1966, 33 "large-capacity tunnel flushers" were fielded with US, ARVN, and Korean forces. These were the Buffalo Turbine Model K, the Mare Generator, and the Resojet. They could be sling-loaded under a UH-1 Huey. Besides flooding tunnels with CS, they were also used to flush out CS and smoke and supply air to tunnel rats. The large-capacity tunnel flushers were operated by divisional- and brigade-level chemical detachments.

Mity Mite blower

The M106 Mity Mite agent dispenser was a commercially made sprayer or duster for agricultural pesticides marketed by Sears Roebuck and Company. It could spray a CS agent just as easily as pesticides. In fact, chemical troops used them to spray mosquito pesticides over firebases. The backpack-carried device consisted of a two-cycle gasoline engine, fuel tank, blower, agent tank, and a 2ft-long disperser hose. It weighed 25lb when empty. One quart of fuel would operate the M106 for just over 30 minutes and displace 450ft^3 of air per minute. The agent tank could hold 10lb of powdered CS or 3 gallons of liquid pesticide.

For use against tunnels, the Mity Mite was set beside a tunnel entrance with additional fuel at the ready. The opening would be sealed with a poncho and its edges held down by shoveled dirt. The hose would then be inserted through the poncho's central head opening and sealed with duct tape. Another method suitable for small entrances was to use the top half of a 5-gallon oil can with a hole cut in the top. This was jammed into the tunnel's entrance and the dispenser hose inserted. The Mity Mite would then be started and CS blown into the tunnel. The air bearing the CS would spread through much of the tunnel system, which is why the VC incorporated airlocks and water locks in their tunnels. The duration of the operation depended on the tunnel system's size. The CS would drive out and in some cases asphyxiate inhabitants, as it displaced oxygen.

Before pumping in CS, colored-smoke grenades were tossed into the entrance and the Mity Mite would then force the smoke through the tunnel to reveal most of the entrances, vents, and firing ports. If the system was so large that the smoke would not spread throughout its full length, the Mity Mite would be reinstalled at an opening farther along and the process begun again. This allowed the tunnel system's rough trace to be plotted. White smoke from AN-M8 grenades and M1A1 smoke pots would likewise be pumped in to drive out the enemy, as it too could asphyxiate if dense enough.

Once the tunnel system's openings were revealed and plotted and then pumped full of CS, the Mity Mite would be used to pump in fresh air. This flushed the CS and smoke out of the complex, allowing tunnel rats to enter. Air would continue to be pumped in once the tunnel rats were underground, in order to help them breathe. Another method of supplying air was to land a helicopter nearby and run an up to 100ft hose from the aircraft's auxiliary generator.

The first use of the Mity Mite in this role was by the ARVN 8th Infantry Regiment, 5th Infantry Division, in the III Corps Tactical Zone in October 1965. This occurred in the Iron Triangle area near Cu Chi 25 miles northwest of Saigon. American advisors oversaw the operation, which proved entirely successful, and the techniques were subsequently adopted by all Free World forces.

An M106 Mity Mite blower operated by a chemical detachment has been set up to flush smoke and tear gas through a tunnel system. (US Army)

CONDITIONS OF SERVICE

Life in a firebase

Tunnel rats' living conditions and daily routine were identical to that of normal soldiers. Indeed, tunnel rats were ordinary soldiers for all intents and purposes; they were unique only in their willingness to enter places that no one else would go. Once they had emerged from their subterranean world, they would seamlessly revert back to "normal" status, and enjoyed no special privileges. If serving as a combat engineer, a tunnel rat would spend much of his time constructing, maintaining, and upgrading firebases (see Fortress 58: *Vietnam Firebases, 1965–73*, Osprey: Oxford, 2007). Rifle companies, too, spent time in firebases, as a battalion's four companies were rotated between base security and offensive field operations. These bases were quickly built and were considered temporary in most cases. Some were in place for just days, others for weeks or months. There were some that were semi-permanent, being positioned along main lines of communication and aiding in securing population centers.

Improvements and repairs were ongoing for as long as the base was operational. All manner of bunkers had to be built and maintained. Artillery and mortar positions, perimeter barbed-wire barriers, Claymore mines, trip flares, helicopter landing pads, internal roads, and drainage systems also needed to be constructed. Much of the labor was done by infantrymen, artillerymen and support personnel, with the engineers assisting. When a base was emplaced, engineer units did much of the initial work with powered equipment and then moved on to other tasks. Some engineers remained for base maintenance, often operating power generators, and were on-call for demolitions and tunnel-exploration work.

Everyone living on the base was involved in perimeter security and base defense. Each man was assigned a fighting position if the base was attacked and had to know how to find his way there in the dark. Perimeter guard duty was rotated, usually with one or two-hour shifts. That involved staying awake and alert and peering into the dark tangle of stumps, limbs, barbed wire, and picket posts. Typically, NCOs constantly made the rounds, ensuring that sentries were awake. Most of the excitement occurred when a trip flare was ignited by a marauding animal. Listening posts might be manned at night outside the perimeter wire, usually by three men with a telephone or radio. In daytime, observation posts might be emplaced farther out. Men also stood radio watch, monitoring the command net. If on a line of communications – a major highway used by both military convoys and civilian traffic – checkpoints would be manned during daylight hours, often in conjunction with ARVN, Regional Force, or National Police personnel.

Besides filling sandbags, building bunkers, and stringing barbed wire, there were other work details. These included trash collection, burning trash outside the perimeter, burning latrine waste; unloading and storing ammunition, rations and supplies delivered by convoy or helicopter; pulling KP (kitchen police) duty, water details, and whatever else the first sergeant could think of. Seldom was a suitable local water source available. Water would instead be trucked in by 1,000-gallon tankers or flown in inside 500-gallon sausage-shaped rubber bladders – known colorfully as "elephant turds" – slung under CH-47 Chinooks. There was little water available for washing clothes or for bathing. There was little in the way of entertainment other than reading, card-playing, and letter writing.

Caves were often found among tumbled boulders. This area has obviously been saturated with tear gas. The white powder-like substance is bird guano. (Tom Laemlein/Armor Plate Press)

Chowing down

In firebases the usual meals eaten were B-rations. These were made up of non-perishable and semi-perishable foods including canned, dried, and dehydrated products. B-rations were issued where field-mess facilities were available, but were not refrigerated. Two or three cooks could prepare meals for 100 men in two hours with gasoline field ranges. The food was not unlike A-rations

LIFE IN A FIREBASE

While an improvement over life on a combat operation, living in a temporary firebase was no picnic. Food was improved and sleeping quarters were out of the weather, but there were endless work details, hours of sentry duty, and occasional mortar and rocket attacks. When a firebase was established it was required that every man sleep under two layers of sandbags by nightfall. Bunkers, especially those that had been occupied for a long time, could be squalid, becoming infested with rats, roaches, and other vermin. Victor M200 rat traps and Daisy Red Rider BB guns were provided for rodent control.

This partly sunken bunker is built of two layers of sandbags and the below-ground walls are revetted by pierced steel plate (PSP) airfield mats and U-shaped barbed-wire pickets. This particular sandbag wall lacks timber reinforcing to bear the weight of the heavy roof timbers, and the three or more sandbag layers placed atop it. An internal framework of 8in. by 8in. timber framing reinforced by 2in. by 10in. diagonal planks might be added later, depending on how long the base remained in place. A heavy caliber near miss, or saturation by prolonged rains could collapse the bunker. Wooden cargo pallets were used as flooring and protected occupants from water seepage, but also provided a hiding place for rats. Folding cots, when available, required an air mattress (known as a "rubber bitch"), as their tautly stretched nylon beds were hard as boards. Camouflaged poncho liners were highly prized, as they provided much warmth. The light-nylon fabric had to be taken care of as it was easily damaged.

Mail call was enthusiastically looked forward to. Every few days a helicopter delivered letters and care packages – candy, cookies, and other treats from home. Care packages were habitually shared with squad buddies. Personal gear was stowed in duffle bags. A tunnel-exploration kit contained within an aviator's kit bag, ready to be used at a moment's notice. Ice, when available, was placed in 5-gallon water cans, and beer and soda cans stowed inside. Beer, though, was scarce on firebases. An M17 protective mask hangs on the wall.

(fresh food), but all meat and fish was canned or dehydrated. B-rations might be supplemented by fresh fruits and vegetables. Cereals, oatmeal, powdered eggs, and powdered potatoes were widely used. If prepared properly, the powdered eggs in scrambled form were not too bad. Mashed potatoes tended to be lumpy. Both canned and dried fruits and vegetables were the same as commercially available canned foods. Beverages included coffee, cold tea, canned fruit juices, and powdered flavored drinks. For bread, centrally located bakeries turned out loafs of bread and B-rations included biscuit, muffin, and cornbread mix, as well as pancake and cake mixes.

Infantrymen and engineers did not spend all their time in remote firebases or out in the boonies on operations. Units rotated through brigade and division bases, where they provided security or served as air-mobile reaction forces. Usually, barracks-type quarters with proper washrooms were available along with PXs (post exchanges), clubs, laundries, outdoor movies, and other amenities.

BELIEF AND BELONGING

Although a tunnel rat had to possess the nerve and courage to squeeze into a tiny, pitch-dark hole in the ground, in general their attitudes toward the wider war in which they fought were the same as any other soldier. Whether volunteers or draftees, tunnel rats held many different views regarding their Vietnam tours. It was an abhorrent injustice to some, an inconvenience to others, and some simply made the best of it. Regardless of whether one was opposed to the war, supported it, or was indifferent, there were few who were concerned with the politics surrounding it. If serving in the Army, they knew that they had to endure exactly 365 days. Vietnam was initially surreal for many, and the shock of entering a strange environment populated with people who seemed totally alien was acute, especially considering the fact that most draftees were still in their teens. Usually, within a short time, a soldier would accept his lot and become comfortable with it. The general attitude was to accept one's fate, stay out of trouble, and do one's job.

Many GIs did not think much of the Vietnamese. Even before arriving in Vietnam they had heard little good about the ARVN. Many of the people seemed unengaged in the war or unsupportive of the government. This was an irritation to many Americans as they were over there risking their lives, enduring great discomfort and taking time out from their lives in the "real world" to help defend *their* country. It was no better in the countryside, where the villagers were literally on the frontline. They had no faith in the government, which was seldom able to protect them. Their culture emphasized loyalty to family and village; beyond that they had little interest. They just wanted to be left alone to raise their families, grow their food, and live their lives in peace. Another problem was simply that Vietnamese culture was so different and strange to American eyes. Of course, the Americans were no less strange to the Vietnamese, especially those living in the countryside. Exacerbating the lack of cultural respect were the types of people that most Americans were exposed to: pimps, prostitutes, bar girls, and drug and porn dealers.

There were other problems within the ranks, which tended to become more serious the farther one got away from the combat troops in the boonies. There were drug problems, race issues, and antiwar attitudes. In some cases there were leadership problems as the war dragged on, exaggerated by poor unit cohesion. It worsened in 1970s as the pace of US troop withdrawal increased. That developed into a simple attitude problem, with soldiers asking why they should give it their all when the politicians had given up on the war.

Besides increased drug use from 1969, which was insignificant before, the extent of disgruntlement and frustration was demonstrated in "fragging" incidents. Fragging was the use of grenades to murder unpopular, abusive, inept, or overzealous officers or NCOs. Fragging was typically a series of incidents, sometimes conducted in a graduated sequence as warnings – a smoke grenade might be tossed into an officer's tent, then a tear gas grenade, a frag grenade without the pin pulled, and finally a frag grenade with pin pulled. The targeted individual usually got the point before the process ran its full course. Fragging was not necessarily limited to grenades. Disgruntled men often took the opportunity to shoot their own leaders during the confusion of combat, where it would be assumed that the victim had been

A tunnel rat peers into a tunnel entrance. A bayonet scabbard is fastened to his right calf by a web strap. Such straps also served to secure baggy pants in order to reduce snagging. (25th Infantry Division Museum)

killed by the enemy. Booby traps were also sometimes used. There are no accurate and complete figures for fragging incidents, and there are a great many officer and NCO deaths of uncertain circumstances. Between 1969 and 1971 there were over 700 fragging incidents reported, though not all resulting in death.

Every war is stressful, taking its mental, moral, and physical toll on soldiers, but the Vietnam War was exceedingly so, with problems not seen to anywhere near as great an extent in previous wars. For the tunnel rat the rigors of combat and the privations of military life were exacerbated by the unique perils of the tunnel they explored.

Into the black echo

A question often asked is why a tunnel rat would volunteer to crawl into a tiny hole, probably occupied by a desperate enemy, and filled with CS, booby traps, vermin, and other perils? They could expect to suffer from claustrophobia, panic, oxygen deprivation, and the possibility of being stuck or otherwise trapped underground. They called it the "black echo," which aptly described the environment. They described their dangerous job as "running the hole."

 SEARCHING FOR TUNNEL ENTRANCES AND AIR VENTS

In the Cu Chi area it was a given that tunnels snaked beneath a village. The challenge was to find them, as the VC had become adept at placing entrances and air vents in the most unlikely places, and were skilled at camouflaging them. Infantrymen conducted an initial sweep though a village, mainly on the lookout for overt activity such as weapons and munitions that weren't hidden underground quickly enough and stay-behind VC, which were usually snipers. They also observed how the villagers behaved. They probed under piles of wood and manure, heaps of discarded materials, large earthenware pots, and clumps of brush. Engineers might be flown in to a nearby landing zone to conduct a closer examination. Since searches might continue in the village for some time, an adjacent LZ would be cleared if none were available. Supplies and equipment would be flown in and any casualties and VC suspects evacuated.

Here, combat engineers bring in a chainsaw and demolitions materials to clear a one-ship LZ beside a village. The Remington Super 75 chainsaw shown here was one of several models used to fell trees for an LZ and slash down brush and bamboo when searching for tunnel entrances. The 1-gallon fuel can held by the central figure holds a 1:16 fuel mixture, with 1 pint of lubricating oil to 2 gallons of gasoline. This same mixture was used in the Mity Mite blower. Slung on the rear man's rucksack frame is an M183 demolition-charge assembly (satchel charge) holding 16 M112 1.1lb C4 charges.

A simple one-man shelter. Such a site might have a tunnel entrance concealed within it. Loose leaves were commonly spread on slit-trench floors, making them less noticeable from the air. (Tom Laemlein/Armor Plate Press)

Few tunnel rats could even answer that question, at least not fully. The reasons were as complex and varied as any man's motivations for volunteering for any dangerous undertaking. Many tunnel rats did the job simply because it needed to be done. Others did it because it was indeed a dangerous and challenging task. They wanted to prove themselves, earn respect or honor, or experience the adrenaline rush. Others went into the ground to meet the enemy face-to-face, to penetrate into the unknown and crawl into the enemy's domain; to play in the enemy's backyard so to speak. Some did it as a lark, thinking it would be a short-lived deal. The reasons were varied and could have been a combination of many things; there were no simple explanations.

Most tunnel rats were volunteers and could "unvolunteer" at any time. The continued stress and pressure of the job, or even some particularly dangerous incident, could cause one to have second thoughts. Anyone doing so would seldom be criticized, especially since few officers had ever ventured down a hole. Most units prohibited officers from entering tunnels. Some tunnel rats, however, did not step out. They feared ridicule or could not admit to themselves they did not have what it takes. Sooner or later they were forced to give it up.

In most cases there was no formal process for volunteering for the duty. Most said that anyone over 5ft 6in. need not apply. Nor were there any training courses within units. Many tunnel rats got their start by simply stepping forward when the platoon leader or company commander asked for volunteers to enter and explore a discovered hole. Often there was no time to wait for engineer and chemical support. They needed to know immediately if there was anyone inside or anything of value to the enemy that could be pulled out or destroyed. There were instances in which unprepared men were ordered to check out a tunnel. This seldom went well. If the tunnel proved to be part of a large complex, engineer support might be called in and the area secured. In the meantime, the infantry would continue to reconnoiter the area in search of additional entrances, vents, caches, fighting positions, and contraband.

Some engineer and chemical units conducted a little informal orientation training, mainly on how to operate the Mity Mite, and were provided diagrams of tunnel complexes for study. For the most part, on-the-job training was undertaken on actual operations. New men served first in the support party above ground, then followed a lead tunnel rat, before finally taking on the lead position themselves. There were support-party men who never had any intension of going into the "black echo."

There is no question that tunnel rats had no shortage of guts. They were awarded with promotions and valor awards, the most common being the Army Commendation Medal for Valor and the Bronze Star for Valor.

ON CAMPAIGN

Tunnel rat "units"

Few soldiers had even heard of tunnel rats until arriving in Vietnam. Even then they were seldom aware of them until possibly seeing them wiggle half-naked into a tiny hole with only a pistol and flashlight. There was no such thing as established tunnel rat units. Tunnel rat teams, sometimes more formally called "tunnel exploration" or "tunnel destruction" teams, were ad-hoc teams assembled from experienced personnel performing their normal duties. They might have been combat engineers, infantrymen, cavalry scouts (if an armored cavalry unit), and even from chemical detachments. Some units designated personnel for the job when needed. Others had small standing teams in the headquarters that would be augmented by other experienced personnel as needed. Inexperienced volunteers would be employed for support.

There was no "standard" organization or strength for tunnel teams. There might be one to four tunnel rats venturing alone underground or accompanied by a backup man (depending on the number of entrances discovered), a few men on the surface at each entrance, and personnel to operate Mity Mite blowers. The surface-support party aided with quickly extracting tunnel rats, passing down necessary equipment, preparing demolition charges, maintaining telephone or verbal contact with the tunnel rat, and plotting the tunnel's course with the information relayed back to them. The infantry provided security at each entrance as well as additional security throughout the village or area. The outer perimeter was also secured by infantry to guard against external counterattack.

Most units used three-man teams, consisting of a supervisor and two tunnel explorers. Some used a five-man team, which was the same as a three-man but with two general-support members, who remained on the surface. The allocation of teams varied between units. Four units heavily involved in tunnel exploration and destruction in the III Corps Tactical Zone in late 1966 recommended the issue of tunnel-exploration kits throughout the corps. This

Tunnel rats bring up an 82mm PM37 mortar. Such heavy and bulky weapons were difficult to haul out of the cramped tunnels. (25th Infantry Division Museum)

Even though part of the camouflage has been removed, this tunnel or shelter entrance demonstrates just how difficult they could be to locate in dense vegetation. (Tom Laemlein/Armor Plate Press)

was not necessarily an indicator of the number of teams fielded, but it gives an idea of how teams were allocated (see sidebar).

The 1st Infantry Division had recommended one tunnel exploration kit per brigade and had in practice spread tunnel rat teams throughout infantry battalions. It was soon found that their employment and level of skill was wanting. The tunnel-exploration and tunnel-destruction mission was given to the division's 1st Engineer Battalion in 1967. Their demolition expertise proved essential.

As many tunnel rats were from specialized engineer and chemical units, the activities and makeup of these units deserves some attention.

Combat engineer battalions

A roughly 950-man combat engineer battalion was assigned to each of the seven Army divisions in Vietnam. There were also 13 non-divisional combat engineer battalions plus combat engineer companies assigned to separate brigades. In Vietnam, combat engineers were capable of constructing simple facilities, repairing roads and bridges, repairing airfields, etc, but most of their efforts were spent on building firebases, airstrips, helipads, installing and repairing barriers around bases, maintaining and repairing roads, clearing helicopter landing zones, and clearing roads of mines. Engineers might also have been attached to rifle companies to handle demolitions, mainly for blasting bunkers, tunnels, and supply caches. They also created small helicopter landing zones to lift out troops, deliver supplies, and medevac wounded men. This was accomplished through the use of explosives, chainsaws, and machetes. Another job was to assist with the extraction of food, munitions, and other material discovered in enemy caches (which were often hidden in tunnels).

Chemical detachments

Divisions and separate brigades were authorized a small chemical detachment. In a conventional environment the detachment operated with

Tunnel rats of the 168th Engineer Battalion prepare to enter a tunnel in the Iron Triangle. Its camouflage and surrounding foliage have been blasted away. An RL-39A field telephone wire reel holding 500ft or wire can be seen to the right. The spiral cord leads to a TA-1/PT sound-powered telephone. The shoulder insignia is of the 18th Engineer Brigade. (Tom Laemlein/Armor Plate Press)

the division command post, advising the staff on chemical warfare and smoke operations, decontamination requirements, and enemy chemical-warfare capabilities. They also coordinated chemical, biological, and radiological reconnaissance and surveys among the division's units. In Vietnam the five-man detachment had little to do other than advise on the employment of tear gas. Often the detachment was expanded to operate Mity Mite blowers and assist with the employment of tear gas against tunnels as well as for area denial. The latter included dropping bulk CS powder from helicopters, spraying both CS and defoliants from helicopters, and firing CS artillery rounds. The detachment did not actually perform the CS delivery, but planned and coordinated its use. Area denial using CS included saturating known enemy base areas, caches, infiltration trails, and abandoned US firebases (to hamper VC scrounging). Detachments operating Mity Mites and other blower systems might include tunnel rats. How these detachments were used and augmented varied much between divisions and brigades. By 1966 most were augmented by a standing tunnel rat team or at least a Mity Mite team. A team operating a Mity Mite was typically made up of the following:

One team leader (an officer or NCO)

One Mity Mite operator (who carried the blower)

One assistant operator (who carried 2 gallons of gasoline, 1 quart of oil, a tool kit, and two ponchos)

Three munitions bearers (who each carried three M1A1 smoke-pots and five M18 colored-smoke grenades)

EXPERIENCE IN BATTLE

The experiences of the tunnel rat varied greatly depending on unit techniques, the terrain, and how the enemy operated, as well as the period in which he served in Vietnam. There were no typical operations. Each had its own unique aspects and dangers.

Tunnel systems might be nothing more than a few feet in length, quite often less than 70ft. Tunnel rats were also often called upon simply to check simple bunkers. This was not because bunker searches were difficult, but because tunnel rats were better prepared to deal with booby traps. Large, sprawling, multi-level tunnel complexes were rare.

A "cherry" tunnel rat

A newly volunteered tunnel rat, if at all possible, would be introduced to the underground world by searching individual bunkers and very small complexes. Of course, when large complexes were discovered he might be forced to take on more challenging searches.

A 25th Infantry Division tunnel rat, assigned to Company D, 2nd Battalion, 27th Infantry, was initiated into his subterranean vocation by searching small bunkers found in an enemy base camp. The entrances were hidden in clumps of brush. The 2ft-diameter shafts were sunk 5–6ft into the ground. Some 2ft above the bottom (the lower part served as a water and grenade sump) was a horizontal shaft running for several feet before making a sharp turn; it then ran a few feet into a chamber large enough to house one or two men. The tunnel rat was lowered by his arms into the shaft and a flashlight and pistol were passed down as he waited for his eyes to adjust and listened for sounds. Even in the entrance shaft it was noticeably cooler. As tunnel rats seldom expected to find such nests occupied, they rarely first dropped in a grenade. That said, any sound or sign of occupation would warrant one being tossed in. Using extreme caution, the tunnel rat would aim his flashlight around the angle of the horizontal tunnel, ready to pull his arm back at a instant's notice. The smelly sleeping chamber would be quickly searched for weapons, ammunition, equipment, and documents.

After searching several such nests, the novice tunnel rat gained more confidence, sometimes leading to overconfidence. Lowered into another shaft, our tunnel rat peered into the tunnel and in the flashlight beam saw a leg. He immediately fired his .45-cal., resulting in a damaged eardrum. Backing out and checking again, he determined that the leg had not moved. With extreme

A crisscrossed log-constructed bunker. The tiny entrance was typical. This made it difficult for Americans to enter and complicated efforts to avoid or detect booby traps. (Tom Laemlein/Armor Plate Press)

caution he checked the VC and found that he was dead from previous wounds. It appeared that he had crawled into the hole and bled to death. Enemy dead were typically left in tunnels and bunkers.

Most tunnel systems were excavated by Local Force VC. Main Force VC and the NVA did not build tunnel systems; tunnels were long-term projects and these groups were mobile combat forces. They used more conventional defensive positions and bunkers. However, tunnels were the only way in which Local Force VC could survive. They had to have facilities, storage sites, and places to hide. One cannot operate and hide in the jungle in one area over prolonged periods of months and even years without being found. Going underground provided an ideal hiding place. They were ideal in the tactical sense, but not for comfort or well being. Life underground was miserable and dangerous, but there were few alternatives. The Local Force's role was to defend and control the villages. They relied on the sympathetic or intimidated villagers for intelligence, food,

Infantrymen light a book of matches to drop down a tunnel entrance shaft to determine its depth. The M17 protective mask case is seen on the left hip of the rightmost man, its normal position of wear. The center man also has a protective mask case. The small pocket was for accessories. (1st Cavalry Division Museum)

A 25th Infantry Division tunnel rat peers around a bend in a cave. He is armed with a .38-cal. Special S&W Model 10 revolver and holds an early version of the MX-991/U right-angle flashlight without the guards protecting the switch. (Tom Laemlein/Armor Plate Press)

and labor. It would be trusted villagers who concealed the entrances when the VC ducked into their tunnels. Fear of retaliation kept most villagers quiet. Once they had concealed the entrance, a procedure they practiced, they would continue on with their daily routine, hoping to appear innocent when Free World troops arrived. They might be tending a garden, carrying firewood down a path, or feeding chickens.

A "routine" day

Tunnels invariably had at least two entrances, to allow escape if one was discovered, plus two or three vents. A great deal of caution had to be used when tunnel rats emerged from an opening other than the one they entered

Troopers of the 1st Cavalry Division cautiously inspect a Vietnamese hooch northeast of Saigon. Even though villagers are present, there are fearful of booby traps and ambushes. (Tom Laemlein/Armor Plate Press)

 UNCOVERING AND ENTERING A TUNNEL

Only one tunnel entrance had to be found initially. This would be carefully uncovered and checked for booby traps. Sometimes a satchel charge would simply be detonated at the entrance to blast away camouflage, blow open any covering material, detonate booby traps, and kill any waiting ambusher. Once exposed, frag and CS grenades might be thrown in, just to make sure. The entrance would then be sealed with a poncho, an M106 Mity Mite blower hose inserted, M1A1 white smoke pots emplaced, and the tunnel flooded with the oxygen-displacing smoke. Besides flushing out the VC, the smoke seeped out of other entrances, air vents, and firing ports. Infantrymen would be placed throughout the area to report any smoke seepage. Additional troops were sent to cover each discovered entrance in order to guard against a breakout. Tear gas flooding through tunnels could force the desperate VC to emerge into withering fire. An M1A1 smoke pot weighed 12lb and burned grayish-white smoke for five to eight minutes after a ten-second delay. Colored-smoke grenades, with less-dense smoke, were used in the same manner. Before a tunnel rat entered the tunnel, the Mity Mite was used to flush out the smoke and tear gas. Besides M183 satchel charges containing 16 1.1lb M112 C4 blocks, entire 46lb cases of C4 with 30 M112 charges were dragged into tunnels, emplaced at key points, linked by detonating cord, and detonated, in order to collapse them. Troops cleared the area for this event. Besides the obvious danger of collapsing tunnels, hidden ammunition stores could be sympathetically detonated, with impressive results.

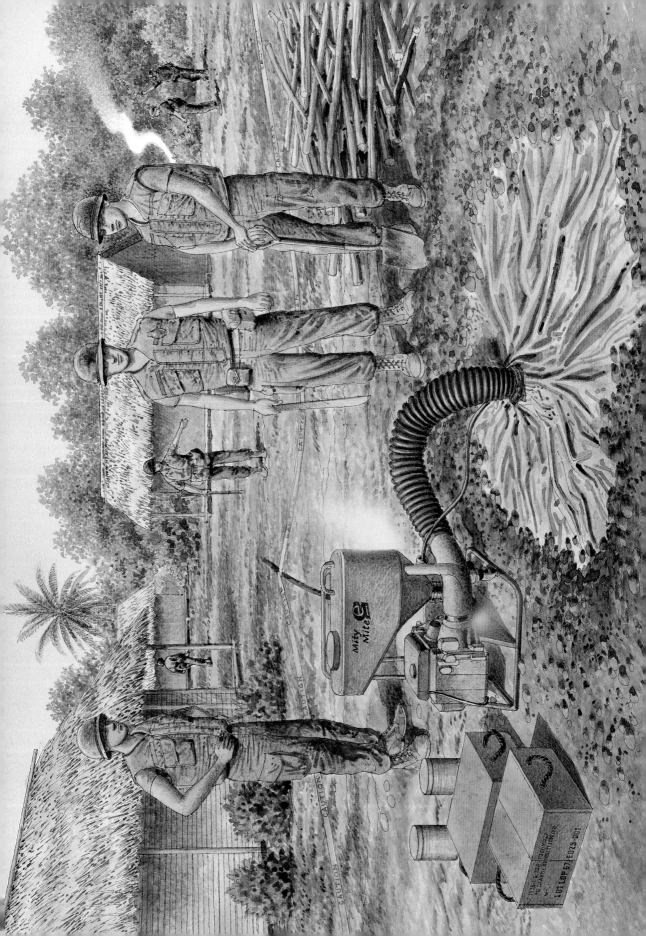

A grinning VC is ordered out of tunnel entrance. This entrance is in an unusually exposed place, with little concealment. It required some effort to place them in less obvious locations. (1st Cavalry Division Museum)

through fear of being shot by friendlies. The entrances and vents were often ingeniously hidden. Small tunnels would also be found on the outskirts of villages in such unlikely areas as cemeteries, cultivated fields, and along riverbanks with underwater entrances.

A typical search-and-clear operation entailed a village being cordoned off, which involved it being surrounded with troops posted to prevent anyone entering or leaving the area. There also had to be a reaction force available in the event of a breakout or an external counterattack. The smaller tunnels found in most villages did not house elaborate facilities, but served only to hide weapons, equipment, food, and the VC themselves.

Villagers would be questioned and a scout dog would make the rounds, as well as infantrymen making visual searches. Sometimes a previously captured VC or a willing informer was brought in to identify entrances. When these small tunnels were discovered, infantrymen would sometimes volunteer to check them out. They may or may not have had previous experience. Some units put together ad hoc tunnel teams with minimal equipment. If the area appeared to be ripe with tunnels, caches, and bunkers, engineer tunnel rats would be called in.

Either way, any discovered entrances and vents were marked and the camouflage removed, whilst always on the lookout for ingenious booby traps. An interpreter or Kit Carson Scout[1] would shout into the tunnel for the occupants to surrender or be grenaded or buried alive. After this, any VC would simply come out with their hands up, sometimes even with sheepish grins. They would be "encouraged" to reveal other tunnels and hidden sites.

[1] These were defected VC who were validated and accepted as *Hoi Chanhs* (ralliers) under the *Chieu Hoi* (open arms) program implemented by the RVN Government in 1963. They were attached to US units and were invaluable as scouts, for locating booby traps and tunnels, and communicating with civilians.

A Vietnamese interpreter questions villagers in hopes of finding out information on the enemy. The location of tunnel entrances was highly valuable information. (1st Cavalry Division Museum)

Even if anyone came out of the tunnel to surrender, the tunnel rat's job was not done. The unimposing entrance might lead to 30ft of tunnel or a massive multi-level complex stretching for hundreds of feet. Even if it was a small tunnel, it had to be searched for anything of value to the enemy. The tunnel was initially explored to determine its extent. If it went beyond 300ft, further exploration was often called off. There simply was not the time or manpower. If a tunnel complex was that large it was usually blasted closed.

If no VC came out of the tunnel, and even after someone did, the entry shaft would be grenaded or a small demolition charge would be dropped in. This not only neutralized any waiting enemy, but detonated or disabled booby traps. If it was suspected that the complex was large enough for the effort, a Mity Mite team would arrive. They would drop in white smoke pots or colored-smoke grenades, seal the entrance to prevent the escape of air and smoke, and begin forcing in air to spread the smoke, thereby identifying other entrances and vents. Once this was accomplished, CS grenades would be dropped in and as the smoke was flushed the CS seeped through the tunnels. These processes could take up to an hour. Before tunnel rats could enter, the blowers were operated for another hour, pumping in fresh air to flush out the remaining smoke and CS. Fresh air might continue to be blown in to aid tunnel rats once they were inside, but more than not often they requested that the blowers be turned off so they could hear the slightest sounds.

The tunnel rat knew that the larger the complex, the more dangerous it was in regards to confronting the enemy and finding booby traps. Crawling into the tunnel, the lead tunnel rat would let his eyes adjust and listen. It would only take one or two angle changes to be in total darkness. Near the entrance with some indirect light available, and he would search for booby traps. This would most likely be in the form of tripwires, but booby traps could come in the form of pressure-activated mines, a detonator under a board or log, or a completely concealed punji stake pit.

A knife or probe was helpful at this point, but having just entered, our tunnel rat held a pistol at the ready and a flashlight in his other hand. He listened. Even though he was wearing an XM28 mask, he could smell the lingering zinc smell of the smoke and burnt CS, and could feel its burning itch on his bare arms. He knew it would progressively worsen. The mask restricted his field of vision, with the flashlight creating a glare. It was also hot, making his face sweat, and was just plain uncomfortable.

He eased forward, moving one hand and one knee at a time. Besides the smoke and CS, he smelled intense mustiness and human waste. It was cool, dry, and dusty. Scanning the floor, walls, and ceiling, he was looking for any signs of booby traps or concealed trapdoors. A knife was on his belt or in his cargo pocket. With close examination, trapdoors might be found by detecting seams, a change of texture, or small piles of crumbled dirt and dust. The latter might be found below vents too. He could also feel moving air near a vent, as the blower was not forcing air down the tunnel. Even if it had been, he might notice warmer air coming into the tunnel at the vent.

This hooch was burned to the ground when a hidden bunker was discovered inside. It appears to have been blasted open by a satchel charge. (Tom Laemlein/Armor Plate Press)

A cross-section of a tree (its underside is shown here) was attached to a hinged frame to conceal a tunnel entrance, making it appear to be a tree stump. (Tom Laemlein/Armor Plate Press)

Behind him was his backup man, another tunnel rat, and a "cherry" just as he had been only a couple of months before. The backup man held a compass and a TA-1/PT sound-powered telephone. Each time they came to an angle change he would give the azimuth (direction) change in degrees to the surface party, along with the estimated distance back to the last angle change. They plotted this on a paper map. It was not precisely accurate, but close enough to get a general idea of the tunnel's course and layout. They also relayed back any features such as side rooms and what they contained, air and water locks, other entrance shafts, vents, and anything of interest. If an entrance could be found on the surface then it would be opened to allow in fresh air and to provide a closer escape route for the tunnel rats. The surface party often moved to this new exit and dropped the phone line in there. This gave the backup man less wire to drag behind him. After even a hundred feet it was difficult to drag, and it became caught on walls and obstructions.

Sounds made by the enemy often led to a halt and a period of prolonged listening. If deep in the complex, it was not considered cowardly for the team to back out, fast. There was nothing to be gained in a blinding, ear-shattering shootout at a few yards' range. It was not worth it to kill one or two of the enemy, or to press on and try to explore more of a tunnel. More importantly, it was not worth getting killed for, which was virtually certain with fire directed down a narrow tunnel.

It was exhausting work demanding the use of all one's senses, and the mental and physical strain was great. The two tunnel rats might periodically exchange positions if they could squeeze past one another.

Detecting a booby trap was a tense moment. It had to be examined closely to determine what it was and how it was triggered. There was always the possibly that it might have two different types of triggers, causing it to detonate when one of them was activated. Grenade arming pins were carried to neutralize booby-trapped grenades. A wire-cutter, side-cutting pliers, or M2 cap crimper could be used to cut tripwires. When bypassing a neutralized booby trap, extra caution had to be used, as it may have been a diversion for a second one just a few feet down the tunnel. More often, especially if deep within the complex, it was advisable to simply leave a

An American-made M26 frag grenade, or "lemon grenade," rigged as a booby trap. It is secured to the stake by trip wire. A safety pin has been inserted into the grenade in order to disarm it. (Tom Laemlein/Armor Plate Press)

Troops inspect a village water well for a hidden tunnel entrance. In the background is an M48A3 Patton tank. (Tom Laemlein/Armor Plate Press)

booby trap alone and withdraw. It was rare if ever for tunnel rats to install their own booby traps. It was too time consuming, they were dangerous to install, and they achieved little.

After two angle changes, each leg being some 15ft long, our two tunnel rats came to a side room. The opening to the right was easily made out as a black patch in the wall. It was reported to the surface. Approaching with

 BOOBY TRAP IN A TUNNEL

The hazards of exploring a tunnel system were numerous, even before taking account of the enemy. There was vermin, dangerous animals and bugs, oxygen degradation, smoke and fumes, residual tear gas, the danger of becoming trapped, and more. The VC sometimes emplaced booby traps, but this was not as widespread as is generally assumed. There was the problem of long-term storage of mechanical and explosive devices in a dusty or wet environment, the amount of time necessary to emplace such traps, and the danger of one's own people triggering it.

The simplest and most rapidly emplaced booby traps incorporated hand grenades, which were readily available. These were usually tripwire-activated. Once such a grenade was activated by pulling the arming pin via a tripwire, after which the arming lever flew off (clearance had to be provided to allow for the lever's arc), the grenade detonated after its normal delay. This was 3.2–4.2 seconds for Soviet/Chinese grenades, and 4–5 seconds for American grenades. This delay time was insufficient to allow a tunnel rat to back out, no matter how alert and quick he was; the fragments and blast over-pressure would funnel down the confined tunnel further than he could move in that short time. Even if he were able to take cover around a turn or sharp angle, the over-pressure would wound or completely disable him. Of course, such booby traps were not emplaced near such cover anyway. Trip wires could be run at any height and angle. Fortunately, trip wires were relatively easy to detect in a flashlight's glow. The tunnel rat shown here is using an Air Force survival knife as a probe and is armed with a .45-cal.

Grenades could be placed in a small hole, usually inside a can, with the pin already removed and the can holding down the arming lever. When the wire was pulled it yanked the grenade out of the can, allowing the lever to fly off. This particular grenade is inserted inside a downward-angled can and held in place by a piece of wood, to which the wire is attached. The grenade would slide out when the wire was tugged. Tunnel rats carried grenade-arming pins to deactivate such booby traps. Further down the tunnel is a punji-stake trap concealed by a mud-covered woven mat. The bamboo stakes, often smeared with excrement to cause infection, could seriously disable a tunnel rat and he would then be difficult to extract from the tunnel.

caution, before moving up to the opening, the surrounding areas were searched for booby traps. With even more caution, the lead man crept up to the opening, quickly shinned the light in and jerked it back immediately. With no reaction from within, he quickly peeked in with the light. After waiting for some seconds he looked in again, slowly sweeping the light through the room, and seeing dark shapes. Taking more time, he worked the light through the chamber, checking the shapes and probing into corners. He swept the ceiling too, noting that it was braced by thick lengths of bamboo.

Anything could be turned up. The author was with a 1st Cavalry Division battalion as a liaison NCO. One of its companies found 50 pairs of A-cup bras, and a several-days-old human left arm in one tunnel. No one even tried to speculate. A few days later another company in the battalion found a bunker with cardboard boxes of brightly colored bikini bottoms. The battalion CO on the radio couldn't stop laughing and asked the company CO if there was right arm in the bunker. The irony was lost on the captain.

Within the side room our tunnel rats found a Chinese-made 57mm recoilless rifle and four crates of ammunition, with four rounds in each. There were also several sacks of rice and a full rucksack. This was reported and they awaited word on what to do. Only the lead man had entered the 4ft by 6ft room. The backup man crept ahead to the next bend, checked it out, and waited with his pistol ready. After a wait that seemed to last forever, the

Infantrymen and an M113A1 APC commander aid in pulling up the wheeled mounting of a 7.62mm SG43 machine gun from out of a bunker. A slit trench serves as a bunker entrance. (Tom Laemlein/Armor Plate Press)

American-produced sacks of grain are brought up from a tunnel by 11th Armored Cavalry Regiment troopers. They would be turned over to RVN Government-controlled villages. Such items were often stolen by stevedores and truck drivers or sold or traded by corrupt government officials. (Tom Laemlein/Armor Plate Press)

telephone told them to bring out the "reckless rifle" (they suspected the CO wanted it as a unit war trophy), the rucksack, which might contain intelligence documents, and the rice. This would support a program in which captured rice was given to RVN Government-controlled villages. There were four 50kg (110lb) sacks. It would be a struggle to get the bulky and heavy bags out, so the tunnel rats reported that there were only two bags. The ammunition was not touched, as it might have been booby-trapped. As the lead man checked the rice, rucksack, and recoilless rifle for booby traps, a support man, a wannabe tunnel rat, came down the tunnel with two lengths of 120ft nylon rope tied together to make a continuous loop. The rucksack was tied to the loop first, because of its potential intelligence value. It was pulled out easily, with the support man working the looped rope around his leg. This way the next item could be tied on and pulled out without having to bring a rope back down the tunnel. The rice bags were next, and proved to be difficult to drag around the tunnel's corners. Lastly came the recoilless rifle, which proved to be extremely difficult to remove, with its many projections digging into the dirt. It had to be worked every inch of the way.

Owing to the time spent dragging the material out of the tunnel, it was decided to emplace demolition charges to collapse it, destroying the ammunition and the remaining rice (the latter of which was unknown to the CO). Two 18lb M183 satchel charges were brought down the tunnel.

A tunnel rat brings canned rations out of an underground supply cache. (25th Infantry Division Museum)

The surface party had precut the length of detcord from the entrance to the side room based on the measurements given by the tunnel rats. One satchel charge was set in the side room with the 57mm ammunition and the other midway between the room and the entrance. Lengths of detcord from the satchel charges were tied onto the mainline detcord with girth hitches with an extra turn. The surface party prepared a third charge about 10ft inside the

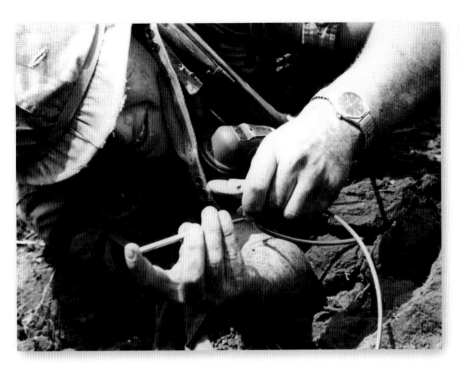

An M7 non-electric blasting cap is crimped to detcord using an M2 cap crimper. (1st Cavalry Division Museum)

entrance and fitted an electric detonator. An electrical firing wire was run out 100ft to a ditch. The rifle platoon leader securing the site was briefed about where the tunnel was and he moved his troops back.

The lead tunnel rat was the last man out, and he double-checked the ties in the detcord. Everyone was ordered to take cover. The 10-cap blasting machine was attached to the firing wire, and the area surveyed to ensure that all was clear. The traditional, "Fire in the hole," was shouted three times. The team leader then twisted the handle on the "hellbox" and the three satchel charges detonated simultaneously with a dull trump. It was felt through the ground and a large clould of reddish dust was blown from the entrance. Dust also puffed from vents and a second entrance farther away. There were whoops of excitement from the troops.

The platoon leader immediately sent a squad to the second entrance and three frag grenades were dropped in once the shattered trapdoor had been completely removed. A CS grenade was tossed in for good measure. As time was short and they had been ordered to search a small base camp discovered a kilometer away, they could not leave this entrance intact.

They prepared another satchel charge, this one with two dual-initiated, 30-second time fuses with a blasting cap on the ends and taped to the free end of detcord in the satchel charge. An M60 fuse igniter was attached to the ends of both time fuses. The area was cleared, an engineer pulled to safety pins from the M60 igniters, shouted the three, "Fire in hole," warnings, yanked the pull rings, igniting the fuses with a low pop, and dropped the charge into the shaft. There was a rough bump felt through the ground, a cloud of dust and smoke was expelled from the hole, and web-like cracks appeared around it. Another method of destroying tunnels was to pump in acetylene gas and detonate it with demolitions.

The full extent of the tunnel was unknown, nor was it known if there was anyone inside. It is likely that there were, but they may have escaped through a connecting tunnel or through a bunker hidden at the edge of the village.

Non-electric demolition kit

The non-electric demolition kit included items issued with the kit plus non-explosive and explosive components that had to be requested separately.

Components issued with basic kit
2x demolition kit canvas carrying bags
2x 10-cap capacity blasting cap boxes
2x M2 cap crimpers
2x pocketknives
2x demolition charge computing tapes

Non-explosive expendable components
20x M1A4 priming adapters
50x M1 detonating cord clips
2x ¾in. black adhesive electrical insulation tape rolls
2x ½lb cans M1 adhesive paste for demolition charges
1x ½pt can waterproof blasting-cap sealing compound

Explosive components (these varied in the field)
50x M7 nonelectric special blasting caps
40x 2½lb M5A1 C4 demolition charges (or 80x M112)
50x M60 waterproof fuse igniters
2x 100ft detonating cord spools
2x 50ft time delay blasting fuse coils
2x M10 universal explosive destructors

A city underground

By far the largest tunnel systems were found in the Cu Chi region in the III Corps Tactical Zone. After realizing the extent of the tunnels, when possible they were explored as fully as time allowed. This proved to be a major effort, and units stayed on the ground for days as the searches, cordons, sweeps, and tunnel exploration went on.

Our tunnel team was assigned a tunnel that had been discovered by an ARVN unit. They had moved on and a US rifle company now provided security. The entrance had been discovered beneath a stack of woven-palm rice-drying mats. Two hours had been spent pumping first CS and then colored smoke through the tunnel. Another entrance had been found under a trash pile of cans, tires, scrap metal, and bottles. Because it was deep under trash that was difficult to remove, it was assessed as an emergency escape hatch. The air vents with violet smoke wafting out revealed that the tunnel stretched at least 200m. Another hour was spent flushing the smoke out. In the meantime the tunnel rats prepared their equipment and demolition charges and talked quietly, awaiting the word to descend into the unknown.

Regardless of the potential size of the complex, entry and exploration started off just as with any other tunnel. After a few turns though, it became

A 40lb cratering charge is dragged into a tunnel by 173rd Airborne Brigade tunnel rats. The amount of detcord indicates that it will be emplaced a good distance inside. (Tom Laemlein/Armor Plate Press)

unpleasant. The air being pumped through the tunnel had at first kept the stench from reaching them, but in a side tunnel they found a half-dozen bodies, maybe two days old. The tunnel rats were ordered to bring them up. They questioned the order, stating the danger of booby traps, but confirmation of body count was more important to some commanders than others.

The tunnel rats in the team agreed to share the grim duty; they would each bring up two bodies. This entailed applying a liberal amount of Vicks VapoRub below their noses, even though they already wore masks, as masks could not keep out odors. Aqua Velva aftershave lotion was used too. After checking the first body as best as possible without moving it, the glove-wearing tunnel rat gingerly tied a rope around the ankles. Even with VapoRub, the stench was sickening and no one was criticized for puking up. The tunnel rat was pulled out and several men gave the rope a heave, but because of the corner turns, the body did not budge. The tunnel rat had to go in and pull the rope from just around the corner from the side tunnel. He tugged at the rope, half expecting a deadly concussive blast, but nothing happened. Working in shifts, they dragged out the bodies. It was disconcerting to some that this would be the same method by which their body might be dragged out, although they might first be placed in a black rubber body bag.

A detailed exploration of this tunnel was possible even with the time spent on recovering bodies. It proved to be 2,300ft in length, with numerous angular turns. The shortest legs were 3ft long and the longest 30ft. The main tunnel was 2ft wide and 2½ –3ft high, mostly with an arched ceiling. Rather than bamboo tube vents, they were conical in shape, a foot across in the tunnel end and 2in. across on the surface. The tunnel was relatively shallow, owing to a high water table; it was near the Song Saigon River, so the vents were 5–7ft in length. About every 100m the tunnel opened into 4ft by 6ft rooms. These were 3ft high with a seating shelf on one side. They were used during bombardments and there was usually a vent present. Similar rooms were found at the end of the six 10–20m long branch tunnels. Large water-filled clay pots were buried in some of these with their mouths flush with the

ABOVE LEFT
A typical shelter chamber inside a tunnel. The main tunnel continues on to the right. The roof is reinforced by braced poles. Palm fronds insulate the floor, which was typical. (Tom Laemlein/Armor Plate Press)

ABOVE
A wider-than-usual tunnel. A side room or tunnel entrance branches to the right side. (Tom Laemlein/Armor Plate Press)

floor. At 30–40m intervals along the main tunnel were short offshoot tunnels with the end walls backed by bamboo lattice work. This was pulled out of one and a loose earth-filled shaft was discovered. This could have been dug out and used as an escape route. Tools were found throughout the complex. Much to the disgust of one novice tunnel rat, who opened one of several US ammunition cans, he found that the airtight container had been used as a chamber pot. These were taken to the surface and dumped and washed out at night.

Booby traps were seldom found deep inside a tunnel; they were too dangerous and troublesome to the occupants. However, one of the side room entrances had a punji stake pit placed so that an intruder would jam a hand or knee into it. One of the experienced tunnel rats found it the hard way, with two barbed bamboo spikes shoved through the palm of his hand. They had to be painfully cut off before he could be moved. With great difficulty he was placed on a folded poncho and dragged out, with two tunnel rats alternating on the exhausting job. It would have been easier to drag him on a body bag as they had web-carrying handles, but many soldiers did not like the idea. On the surface he would be given morphine and placed on an antibiotic IV, as it was common for feces or rotting meat to be smeared on punji stakes.

H TUNNEL EXPLORATION

A US unit secures the area around a tunnel entrance discovered in a rice-storage shed. A tunnel rat has entered the shaft while the support party on the surface prepares to assist him. Concealed trapdoors hide storage rooms and the tunnel entrance in the false water-well shaft. The water well also serves as a water trap to block tear gas, smoke, and concussion blasts. It might also discourage further exploration. Two bamboo air vents can be seen, their openings hidden in brush. The Local Force VC would take refuge in the tunnels and hide along with their supplies and munitions. It was the ultimate cat and mouse game. Tunnels might be multi-level, with concealed trap doors, dead ends, false walls, booby traps, and side rooms. Besides securing the area while the tunnel-exploration team did its job, the infantrymen searched for additional entrances, air vents, fighting positions, and contraband. They also questioned villagers. This was as much to measure the attitude and loyalty of the villagers as it was to find information on the VC, of which they would reveal little or nothing.

A 25th Infantry Division tunnel rat emerges from a village bomb shelter. All villages possessed these for the protection of the inhabitants, and they were not necessarily used by the enemy. Nonetheless, they had to be searched. He holds an M7 bayonet used for probing. (Tom Laemlein/Armor Plate Press)

There was a good chance that the wounded tunnel rat, even if his injuries healed properly, would have been in his last "black echo." The amount of stress endured was high. It was easy for even experienced tunnel rats to lose their nerve, or feel that the odds had turned against them. They were seldom criticized if they shouted, "Pull me out!" It was their decision. Only they could assess what they were dealing with. A man could simply panic without warning, no matter how many times he had run a tunnel. Only he knew when he needed to find a new line of work. Sometimes, men went back to it after a break.

AFTERMATH OF BATTLE

Regardless of the inherent dangers, tunnel rat casualties were surprisingly light. Men did die in fierce hand-to-hand fights below ground, suffocate, drown, or become killed or maimed by booby traps. The mental stress was great, and post-traumatic stress disorder (PTSD) is not uncommon among former tunnel rats. However, it is probably not experienced at any greater percentage than other Vietnam combat veterans. Tunnel rats did suffer more exposure to CS and smoke than many other soldiers. Heavy and prolonged exposure to CS could cause complications if individuals later suffered from asthma and other respiratory illnesses. There is little evidence of this, however. Exposure to HC

A VC killed while fleeing into a bunker. This bunker was emplaced among reeds along a riverbank. (Tom Laemlein/Armor Plate Press)

(zinc-hexachloroethane), the compound used to make white smoke, can cause complications, specifically late-onset pulmonary fibrosis. It contains zinc, which is harmful to lungs. Tunnel rats may have been exposed to vermin and other filth in the course of their duties, but probably suffered from no more than other field soldiers. Field life in Vietnam was unsanitary no matter what precautions and efforts one undertook.

Every soldier looked forward to the magical DEROS – Date Estimated Return from Overseas (pronounced "Dee-roes"). This was set at 365 days starting from the day he left the Continental United States. Even if delayed en route before reaching Vietnam, the countdown had begun. The halfway point was a milestone and often somewhat depressing, with as much time ahead of a soldier as he had behind him. Many men maintained a "short-timer calendar." This might have been a line drawing of a South Vietnam map, a provocatively shaped and clad girl, or a helmet atop boots divided into 365 numbered segments, each colored in or marked with a cross at the day's end.

If a soldier had less than five months remaining before his Estimated Time of Separation (ETS) – the projected date for his release from active duty – he was eligible for early separation. Typically a conscript undertook four to five months of BCT and AIT, a one-month pre-deployment leave, and 12 months in Vietnam. There might have been lag time between the stages of training. By extending for another one to three months in Vietnam they

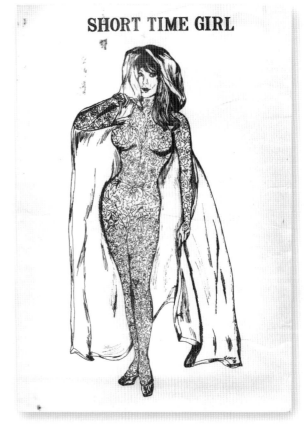

A typical short-timer calendar. Soldiers colored in or crossed off the numbered segments counting down to the day they left Vietnam and returned to the "real world." (VN Center and Archive, Texas Tech University)

SHORT TIME GIRL

An exhausted 25th Infantry Division tunnel rat emerges from accomplishing a physically and mentally demanding mission in the Hobo Woods. (Tom Laemlein/Armor Plate Press)

would be discharged immediately upon return to the United States. Many accepted this option rather than taking a short leave and then doing his remaining few months at a boring stateside post.

All soldiers, whether three-year volunteers or two-year conscripts, were obligated to a total of six years' service. They would be assigned to the Reserve Reinforcement Group for the remainder of their six years. This was a "paper assignment," making them available for recall if necessary, but this would occur only if something along the lines of a world war broke out. In so far as is known, no such reservists were recalled. Upon completion of their six-year obligation they would then be discharged from service. They could opt to join the Army Reserve or Army National Guard.

There is little mention of tunnel rats in unit histories. Since there were no tunnel rat units as such, they being ad hoc teams and volunteering individuals, there are few separate studies and reports other than those buried within unit records.

Other than the 1986 *The Tunnels of Cu Chi* by Tom Mangold and John Penycate, little has been done to chronicle the exploits of the tunnel rats. A B-movie, *1968 Tunnel Rats*, released in 2009 and filmed in South Africa, is an exaggerated and improbable story of tunnel rats, providing a totally unrealistic view of their experiences.

There are no tunnel rat memorials, museums, or associations, at least in the United States. There is an active Vietnam Tunnel Rats Association in Australia (www.tunnelrats.com.au). Even the US Army Engineer Museum at Fort Leonard Wood, Missouri, has almost no information or displays relating to the tunnel rats.

BIBLIOGRAPHY

FM 5-25, *Explosives and Demolitions*, May 1967

Foster, Randy E. M., *Vietnam Firebases, 1965–73*, Osprey: Oxford, 2007

Grant, Mickey (director), *The Cu Chi Tunnels*, Gia Phong Film Studios, 2001

Hanesalo, Bruce A. (ed.), *Tunnel Warfare, Vol. 4: Asian Tunnel Warfare*, Military/Info Publishing: Golden Valley, MN, 1996 (available at http://www.military-info.com/Index.htm)

Lanning, Michael Lee, and Cragg, Dan, *Inside the VC and the NVA: The Real Story of North Vietnam's Armed Forces*, Ballantine Books: New York, 1992

Mangold, Tom, and Penycate, John, *The Tunnels of Cu Chi*, Presidio Press: Novato, CA, 1986

MacGregor, Sandy (as told by Jimmy Thompson), *No Need for Heroes: The Aussies who discovered the Viet Cong's secret tunnels*, Calm Proprietary Ltd: Sydney, 1993

McCoy, James W., *Secrets of the Viet Cong*, Hippocrene Books: New York, 1992

Rottman, Gordon L., *US Army Infantryman in Vietnam 1965–73*, Osprey: Oxford, 2005

——, *Vietnam Infantry Tactics*, Osprey: Oxford, 2011

Stanton, Shelby L., *The Rise and Fall of an American Army: U.S. Ground Forces in Vietnam, 1965–1973*, Presidio Press: Novato, CA, 1985

——, *U.S. Army Uniforms of the Vietnam War*, Stackpole Books: Harrisburg, PA, 1989

INDEX